The Gr

Game of

Maryland

Politics

Other Books from *The Sun*:

Gaining A Yard: The Building of Baltimore's Football Stadium

Raising Kids & Tomatoes

Motherhood is a Contact Sport

The Wild Side of Maryland: An Outdoor Guide

The 1996-1997 Maryland Business Almanac

Cal Touches Home

This *Sun* book was published by SunSource, the information service of the *Sun*. To order any of the above titles, or for information on research, reprints and information from the paper's archives, please call 410.332.6800.

THE GREAT
GAME OF
MARYLAND
POLITICS

BARRY
RASCOVAR

WITH EDITORIAL CARTOONS BY
MIKE LANE

THE BALTIMORE SUN

Published by
 The Baltimore Sun
A Times-Mirror Company
501 N. Calvert Street
Baltimore, MD 21278

Layout and design by Jennifer Halbert
Cover photo by Jim Burger
Edited by Joseph R.L. Sterne

ISBN – 0964981998
Library of Congress Catalog Card Number 98-0704091.

The Great Game of Maryland Politics: a publication of the
Baltimore Sun - 1998 - Baltimore, MD: Baltimore Sun Co: 1998

To Roy and Bette,
Who put me firmly on this road,

And to Ceal,
Who keeps me there

Contents:

Acknowledgements

Ever since its founding in 1837, The Baltimore Sun has been this state's major voice on matters political. Especially in this century, columnists such as H. L. Mencken, Frank R. Kent, Tom O'Neill, Brad Jacobs, Lou Panos and Pete Kumpa have amused and informed Marylanders about the perorations and maneuverings in Washington, Annapolis and City Hall.

The columns in this book are part of that tradition.

A special debt of gratitude is owed to Mike Lane, a first-rate cartoonist and a longtime Baltimore Sun associate. He spent hours culling the best illustrations for this book from 20 years of his editorial cartoons on the Maryland political scene.

Lisa LoVullo, director of electronic news and information services at the newspaper, also warrants special praise for not letting her initial skepticism stop her from seeing the value in publishing this book.

At Sunsource, Jennifer Halbert proved invaluable as a production partner. Her sunny disposition, good judgment and computer skills made work on this project always pleasant. Jim Burger's artistic talents were put to the test to come up with a cover for the book while the State House in Annapolis underwent exterior renovation. As always, he did not disappoint. Debbie Golumbek and Laura Gamble made this undertaking practically painless.

Joe Sterne, who edited these columns and wrote the introduction, deserves all the credit (or blame) for them. It was his idea to have me write a weekly analysis of politics in the state capital — and then gave me a free hand in shaping the column over two decades.

Finally, a thank-you goes to all those writers, editors and publishers at The Baltimore Sun who have made my career so fulfilling and rewarding. There is no better job in life than working for a newspaper. I know my colleagues share that sentiment.

— Barry Rascovar
Baltimore, Md.
September, 1998

Introduction

by Joseph R.L. Sterne

Let's begin with Harry R. Hughes in the early 1980s. The governor of Maryland, after meeting with the editorial board of The Baltimore Sun, says he wants to speak to the editor alone in his office. My desk is messy, as usual, but Harry doesn't seem to notice. He is a very angry guy. The gist of his message is that Barry Rascovar is out to destroy his administration with one negative column after another. And if I would only crack down on my closest colleague, the fellow who really holds the editorial staff together while I worry about nuclear weaponry, then maybe Governor Hughes could tend to governance in a better frame of mind.

My response is the refuge of all editors, i.e., I don't intend to censor the best political columnist in Maryland and, if I did, the publisher of the day would be justified in giving me the boot. Harry storms out. On rare occasions when I see him these days, the sound of gritting teeth is audible.

Now let's go to the circus years of William Donald Schaefer. He'd be caught dead rather than lower himself to a personal visit to the editorial page editor of a newspaper that is so mean to him. Actually, Schaefer got the kind of favorable commentary most politicians would kill for. But you wouldn't know it. For Don Schaefer, the scribbled note (my favorite: "Sterne you stink") or the expletive-filled phone call is the preferred means of communication. Why, he demands, don't I fire that no-goodnik who torments him with his Sunday column and his negative editorials? He can't even bring himself to utter Barry's name. Instead, he refers to a mysterious character named "Curly," which I find rather curious in view of Rascovar's advancing baldness.

Finally, as my long career at *The Sun* sputters to a close, the last governor who has to coexist with both Barry Rascovar and Joe Sterne appears on the scene. He is that most uncuddlesome of politicians, Parris N. Glendening, whose ardent attempts to honeymoon with Barry are predictably (and mercifully) short-lived. Once, on a visit to the fortress on Calvert Street,

Glendening became part of a long and honorable tradition by demanding that I throttle Rascovar. "I don't believe a word he writes," Parris fulminates. Which might be true. But then he adds, "I don't read him anymore," which is an outright fib. The fact is that every Maryland politician worthy of the name reads Rascovar. The pols may not like what Barry has to say, but they damn well need to know what he has to say. His column is the most influential in the state. This is due not only to *The Sun's* giant-sized presence on the Maryland scene; it is because Rascovar is the best source for any reader who wants to know what is really going on in state politics.

Barry is that rare newsman who really knows his Maryland history and the men and women who are making it contemporaneously. He is willing to schmooze with politicians for hours on end. His many sources are varied and reliable. His judgment is rarely wide of the mark. His writing is succinct and no-nonsense, though sometimes laced with juicy irony. He believes government can be a source for good, and insists upon it.

The retired chief judge of the Maryland Court of Appeals, Robert C. Murphy, says he knows "of no other journalist whose columns I have more enjoyed reading and from which I have so greatly profited." Among Barry's strengths, he adds, is "his consistent fairness."

Congressman Ben Cardin calls the Rascovar column "a must read for anyone in Maryland politics." "I have not always agreed with him, but he is certainly thought-provoking," Cardin asserts. "Barry knows all the players and his column is full of news, gossip and possible scenarios that often turn a dull Sunday morning into a hastily arranged conference call among Maryland officials."

Western Maryland College Professor Herbert C. Smith, an expert on Maryland politics, defines Rascovar as "a dependable source of uncommon common sense [who] consistently refuses to suffer fools gladly. Recipients of Rascovar's barbs invariably deserved them and those politicians he praised earned those kudos as well."

H. Furlong Baldwin, chairman of Mercantile Bank & Trust, says Rascovar's work "has gone from a very immature start, without any understanding of economic matters, to a mature and responsible stage." His columns now are "interesting, thoughtful, well-written and frankly more direct than many editorial page writers are willing to be under their own by-line."

Joseph A. De Francis, president of the Maryland Jockey Club, contends that what sets Rascovar apart is "his almost insatiable appetite for facts. Facts form the foundation for separating rhetoric from reason in political analysis, and the conclusions or opinions expressed in Barry's columns have always been built upon solid factual foundations."

There are plenty of accolades for Barry and his column when Maryland political officials are asked for their assessments. "A fine-honed, incisive political mind, as well as a dry sense of humor," says State Senator F. Vernon

Boozer. "His works mirror the real breadth of the political scene – egalitarian to egocentric, profound to trivial, selfless to selfish, saints to sinners," comments State Senator Robert R. Neall.

Former Delegate Timothy F. Maloney describes Barry as "unfailingly honest, incisive and thoughtful... Some of his ideas end up in the State Code and the budget — others on the cutting room floor." Former Elections Board administrator Gene M. Raynor considers Rascovar "a completely selfless political observer and totally honest, a model of integrity [whose] only interest is good government." Giant Food vice president Barry Scher notes that Rascovar is "no patsy" for one of *The Sun's* biggest advertisers. "When we are wrong, Barry lets us know it."

There are criticisms as well (and I'd be worried if there weren't). Peter A. Jay, for many years a conservative voice on *Sun* op-ed pages, complains that while Barry is knowledgeable and calmly authoritative, his "liberal" column contains "regular references to 'right-wing people and policies' but no left wing has yet been identified."

William S. Ratchford, former chief fiscal adviser to the General Assembly, believes that Rascovar has become "an advocate of strong executive leadership [because] over the years he gradually lost confidence in the ability of legislative bodies to carry out their responsibilities." As a result, says Ratchford, "his standard for legislative action was not possible to achieve."

Two Washington area politicians, Tim Maloney and former Delegate Devin J. Doolan, complain that their part of Maryland is short-changed because Rascovar is too focused on Baltimore. "I am reminded," Maloney says, "of that famous *New Yorker* cover where Manhattan dominates the world – only Charles Street looms across Maryland in the Rascovar version." Doolan, after lauding Rascovar, cites Barry's "prejudice for the City of Baltimore – his field of dreams."

Delegate John S. Arnick of Baltimore Country comments that even though Rascovar "misinterprets" at times, he "generally translates well." "One of the real talents of politics and political writing is to get the 'stuff' from the extremes and then go to the middle and blend it all with intelligence," Arnick remarks. "I feel he does that pretty well."

Former Delegate Gary Alexander, who was in charge of the Legislative Follies for years, recalls that Barry, as chief roaster in 1997, turned out to be an accomplished humorist whose whimsy ought to be used more often to "lighten up" his columns.

Maryland Senate President Thomas V. Mike Miller Jr. provides his own unique commentary: "Regardless of which side of an issue you find yourself on, Barry Rascovar's column always provides an insightful perspective and frequently adds fuel to an already contentious debate. Unabashedly pro-Baltimore, Rascovar is never afraid to speak up and speak out on even the most difficult and devisive issues. Or, when it suits his purpose, to use voices from the sewer that are often times totally inaccurate. However, along with scores of other elected officials and countless politicial junkies I faithfully turn to read Rascovar's comments prior to scanning the front page, metro section, or even checking the box scores. A persuasive journalist, his column has helped, in no small way, to mold and shape Maryland politics over the years."

And then there is William Donald Schaefer. "Barry Rascovar?" writes the former mayor and governor and would-be state comptroller. "Yes, I've known him and hated him for those nasty columns and editorials he wrote about me. Over a period of time, the editorials and columns faded from my memory and I got to like the guy. He put me on the pan for years and I tried every way I could be get back at him.

"He expressed his opinions as he saw them," Schaefer continues, "He was of the newspaper philosophy that you are being paid to do your job and not to be patted on the back. He always expected you to do more at one time than was possible. Barry's motives, now that I look back, were to keep you on the straight and narrow and to be a political watchdog... Excellent writer, a thinker, but has little trust of people in public life."

What gives Rascovar special clout is his authenticity. Born in Baltimore on April 19, 1946, he is about as "Maryland" as you can get. Not only did he graduate from Forest Park High School (the celebrated venue for "Grease") but his parents and uncle did as well. The family ran a dry cleaning business at Cold Spring Lane and Dolfield Avenue. To attend college, Barry strayed north of the Mason-Dixon Line – but not by much. He chose Dickinson in Carlisle, Pa., because it was only a few hours from Baltimore.

After picking up a newspaper-entry permit at the Columbia University Graduate School of Journalism in New York, Rascovar in 1969 got a coveted job on *The Sun* – and was promptly assigned to the police districts as was the fate of cub reporters in those days. He had wanted to be a newspaperman since a seventh grade assignment required close reading of current events. His father, a closet Republican, and his mother, a liberal Democrat, often talked politics around the dining room table. After learning the ropes as a reporter covering Baltimore City Hall and the Maryland State House, he was named news editor of *The Sun's* Washington Bureau.

This proved to be a turning point. Rascovar was unimpressed by the much-vaunted Washington press corps. As he tells it now, he found Washington too impersonal, too remote, too much a mad chase after the same story by hundreds of reporters without real access to newsmakers. Conversely, in covering city and state government he was able to get to know politicians personally and to find out what was truly going on behind the scenes. It was just a matter of time before he came back to Baltimore as deputy editorial page editor and chief political columnist 19 years ago.

Though such assorted characters as Harry Hughes, Don Schaefer and Parris Glendening might find this hard to believe, Barry Rascovar really likes politicians. "As a class," he says, "they are extremely human and vulnerable to human foibles." They are entertaining, fun to watch, the stuff of good copy and, above all, they perform valuable services. When he writes something critical of a politician, it does not disappear unnoticed into the Washington ether. Instead, it is likely to get one of these "extremely human" creatures blazing mad and eager to confront the writer of such blasphemy. "The heat," says Rascovar, "can be very uncomfortable."

The pages that follow take the reader on a two-decade tour of Maryland politics, as reflected in a selection of 81 of the 800-plus columns Barry Rascovar wrote over a two-decade period. For some it will be a nostalgia trip; for others, a primer on Maryland politics and practice. The cartoons of *The Sun's* Mike Lane, a trenchant observer of the Maryland scene, add spice and visual relief. On a personal note, permit me to describe Barry Rascovar as a loyal friend and an outstanding newspaperman. From this ink-stained wretch, there can be no greater praise.

Joseph R.L. Sterne joined The Sun *in 1953 as reporter, then moved on to become a foreign corespondent and assistant Washington Bureau chief. In 1972, Sterne was appointed Editorial Page Editor of* The Sun, *a position he held until retiring in 1997.*

A tsunami struck Maryland in late 1978, a powerful political tidal wave the likes of which had never before visited the Free State. After years of publicized corruption trials, voter outrage welled over on election day, sweeping out the remnants of former Governor Marvin Mandel's old b'hoy network. Into the governor's office walked Harry Roe Hughes, telegenic, well-versed in state affairs but a virtual unknown just a few months earlier. His mandate: clean up the mess and put state government back on the straight and narrow.

That he did, but in a way few would have imagined. Harry Hughes, a native of the conservative Eastern Shore, did not believe in exercising the enormous leverage of power that Maryland's governor possesses. He felt that governors should run the bureaucracy and legislators should be left alone to make the laws.

Thus the Hughes years gave Marylanders an era of quiet competence in which power gravitated from the governor's office to leaders of the Maryland General Assembly. Meanwhile, the state and its chief executive experienced good times and bad as the national economy went on a wild roller-coaster ride through recession and prosperity.

Only at the tail end did a major crisis arise – a financial debacle that presaged a far broader national calamity. Ultimately, this proved Harry Hughes' undoing. But that lies years ahead as we begin, barely 12 months after the new Democratic governor took the oath of office...

Chapter 1

The
Quiet
Years

30 Years and $15 Million Later

Annapolis, January 14, 1980

Week No. 1 of the 1980 General Assembly session mercifully is now history. Much like baseball's Grapefruit League, the Assembly uses its initial meetings as spring training for the upcoming season — sharpen the vocal chords, work on hitting those verbal curves, fielding those tricky parliamentary short-hops, and picking up those signals flashed by the coaches.

If you're looking for feverish excitement and frenetic activity, come back in April when the rush to adjournment makes the State House resemble the last days of a tight pennant race. Right now, the pace is leisurely and everyone is in a good mood.

I had missed a number of recent legislative sessions, and, like an old baseball fan, was anxious to return to the ballyard to see what had changed. Not much, as I found out. There was Fred Malkus, red-faced and white-maned as ever, inveighing on the Senate floor against the press, the government and those threatening his rural way of life. There was Jack Lapides, Bolton Hill's pesky iconoclast, provoking yet another Malkus eruption of righteous indignation. And there was the House of Delegates in its usual state of raucous summer camp decorum as it hooted, howled and guffawed at the first opportunity.

So little had changed in my three-year absence (aside from some unfamiliar faces, many of them women) that I wondered how the 1980 version of the General Assembly differs from, say, the 1966 version, or the 1950 version. After picking the memories of veterans of past legislatures, two themes emerged.

One was that these legislators are better educated and more inquisitive than their predecessors. This has made life more strenuous for lobbyists, who no longer can depend on a few powerful lawmakers to deliver the votes. Yet while the legislative process is admitedly more democratic, it also has become more unwieldy and undependable. The governor and the leadership cannot "control" the Assembly. It takes a broader consensus to reach agreement. Far more dramatic have been the physical changes. In past times, the legislature was the stepchild of state government. Now it has grown up, gotten married and moved into its own house. The General Assembly used to be a close-knit family. All the offices were in some nook of the State House or the old Court of Appeals building. Everyone from secretaries to senators was on a first-name basis. Most people took a room for the session at Carvel Hall and spent their nights in the local saloons.

Not any longer. Many legislators forego nightlife action to commute back to spouses and children. Tens of millions of dollars have been spent on huge legislative buildings to give the Assembly its own identity. The cast of supporting characters is enormous.

Janet Hoffman, now the city's influential lobbyist, remembers her first session 30 years ago. She was then a staff member of the legislature's fiscal research division. Actually, she was the entire staff. In those days, there were no legislative secretaries or committee aides. So Ms. Hoffman simply sat in the back of the old Senate Finance Committee room sending notes to the panel's chairman, a 36-year old senator from Calvert County named Louis Goldstein.

Now look at today's situation. The legislature will spend more this year on stamps ($53,940) than it did on fiscal research in 1950 ($40,000). The General Assembly's entire budget for 1950 was $473,000. This year's budget request took 170 pages to explain and totaled $125,600,000. Full-time staff numbers 533. There is a phalanx of bill-drafters, budget analysts, fiscal advisers, commitee aides and secretaries. The legislature has its own printing shop, with banks of computers. It has its own postmistress. The telephone bill runs to $289,600.

Yet there are those who feel something has been lost in the transition from a small, clubby legislature to a mechanized, modernized government operation. The place is awash in paper, lawmakers are deluged with work and it becomes more difficult each year to get an uncomplicated bill through the legislative meat-grinder.

Big isn't always best, as California Governor Jerry Brown is fond of saying. The legislature somehow managed to get the job done in 1950, even if it lacked today's conveniences. But those were simpler times, when there was less pressure to address every social need. The 1980 General Assembly faces a far more complex world, which has neccessitated a drastic overhaul of the way things are done in Annapolis.

Restless Natives

February 4, 1980

There are drumbeats coming from the first floor of the State House and the message isn't a friendly one. Some of the natives are restless and are once again murmuring dark things about Governor Hughes and his patronage aide, Louise Keelty.

If this sounds like a familiar refrain, it is. The situation became so messed up last year that blocs of legislators marched on Mr. Hughes' office. They weren't being consulted. They had been treated rudely. They had been cut off from the appointments process.

The message got through to the governor, who finally sat down with Ms. Keelty and told her that things hadn't worked out. Sometime after this legislative session she will leave the governor's staff, but that won't be soon enough for some lawmakers.

The rap against Ms. Keelty, a Baltimore lawyer active in liberal politics, is that she can be abrupt, abrasive and uncooperative, that she rewards her political friends and allies and deals with legislators as little as possible. The problem, though, is deeper than that and will not disappear when Louise Keelty leaves.

"Louise took Harry literally when she came aboard," said one insider. "She came in convinced that Harry was serious about doing things differently." This meant running the appointments operation like a personnel office, with a minimum of politics.

For the first time in years, cabinet secretaries were consulted about appointments to boards in their departments. The composition of the boards was examined as to race, sex, occupations and geographic representation. For those seeking reappointment it mattered little who your political godfather was; what mattered were the number of board meetings you attended, your activity on the board, and whether you had been judged to have done a good job.

This came as a shock to a good many lawmakers, who had been accustomed to getting their fair share of patronage from past administrations. One city senator said that Ms. Keelty has talked with him only twice about appointments — both times after the individual, from the senator's district, had already been choosen.

This unusual approach may be good government, but it makes for bad politics. "I'm afraid Harry's going to end up losing some bills down here. That's the only way we can get his attention," the senator said.

Exactly how much trouble the governor may have this year will be known February 15, when Ms. Keelty marches into the ornate Senate chamber carrying a green felt bag with the list of appointments.

There aren't many controversial positions this year — chairman of the Workman's Compensation Commission, a seat on the Public Service Commission, another on the Thoroughbred Racing Board, four spots on the Univeristy of Maryland's board of regents and adjutant general of the Maryland National Guard — but there are lots of minor posts to fill.

"For each friend we make with an appointment, we make ten enemies," Ms. Keelty said. The problem is especially sticky on local appointments to school boards and liquor boards. Since his inauguration, Mr. Hughes has made nearly 1,500 appointments for every post from poet laureate to a member of the Worcester County bingo commission.

Without question, the governor has made dramatic strides in selecting blacks and women to fill state posts. Ms. Keelty discovered that the Mandel-Lee administrations hadn't even kept lists of the number of blacks and women given jobs.

But the Hughes administration has had an abysmal record in handling the pure politics of the appointments process. More than anything else, this comes down to a lack of communications. After all, there are few plums left in the Green Bag these days. Senators and delegates tend to become docile if egos are massaged and ruffled feathers are smoothed by an understanding governor. They like to be consulted on appointments, even if it concerns the state boiler rules board or the forestry board. They like to think they have power.

Until Mr. Hughes gives legislators the attention they feel they merit, he will continue to run into trouble. He and his staff are not doing enough handholding to satisfy the lawmakers. Try as he might, the governor can't remove politics entirely from the appointments process.

Louise Keelty practices law in Timonium.

What Conflict of Interest?

March 3, 1980

The late Joseph J. Staszak, a bear of a man with tremendous political muscle in East Baltimore politics, had a way with words. Direct, brief and bluntly honest. "The Senator," as they called him even after he gave up his legislative seat, served only two terms here. But he has gone down in the annals of Senate lore for a remark that rings so true that State House types still wince at its mention.

Among his many business ventures, "the Senator" owned a bar on Dundalk avenue — Joe's Tavern. During the late stages of the 1973 session, the normally taciturn Senator Staszak became the vocal floor-leader for a bill banning cut-rate liquor stores. Unmentioned in the debate was that tavern owners, such as Mr. Staszak, stood to profit handsomely if discount liquor stores disappeared.

Two reporters rushed up to him after the bill had passed. What about the ethical propriety of your actions? Won't you benefit personally from this bill? Aren't you guilty of a conflict of interest? Joe Staszak cut the reporters off with his now famous response:

"How does this conflict with my interest?"

Conflicts between the public's interest and a legislator's personal interest are not new. They have been around Annapolis for as long as there has been a General Assembly. This is, after all, a body composed of citizen-legislators.

For three months each year, 188 Marylanders put on their hats as senators and delegates, and conduct the legislative business of the state. The rest of the year, they are private citizens, trying to earn a living like you and me. Farmers. Teachers. Lawyers. Housewives. Realtors. You name an occupation, and it's likely there's an expert in the General Assembly.

That's the good side of a part-time legislature. "You want people who have involvements and interests," said one lawmaker. "We all have certain conflicts that we can't divorce ourselves from. That's representative government. You don't want people voting in a vacuum." At the same time, you don't want people voting their own interests. Over the years, attempts to deal with the conflict-of-interest issue have been feeble, at best. Fallout from the Spiro Agnew caper led to financial disclosure requirements for public officials. Fallout from the Marvin Mandel melodrama provided impetus for the Maryland Public Ethics Law of 1979. Despite its lofty-sounding title, the new ethics law doesn't accomplish much. It sets out provisions for disclosing possible conflicts. But once a legislator has done so, he can go right on pursuing his private interests by filing a "disclaimer" stating that he will maintain his fairness and objectivity.

John Hargreaves, the deep-voiced delegate from Caroline County, is the most recent legislator to avail himself of this provision so he can continue to advocate higher truck-weight limits. Mr. Hargreaves owns more than $144,000 in stock in Maryland's biggest trucking company.

Mike Miller, a Prince George's County senator, did the same thing before supporting a bill raising interest rates banks can charge on credit cards and consumer loans. Mr. Miller is on the board of directors of the Bank of Brandywine.

Larry Levitan persuaded his fellow Montgomery County senators to give a speedy burial to a bill curtailing tax breaks for Montgomery's posh country clubs. Mr. Levitan is a member of one of the most exclusive of these clubs and stood to see his dues increased by hundreds of dollars.

There are countless examples, like the five members of the House Economic Matters Committee with liquor interests who must sit in judgment on a bill allowing supermarkets to obtain beer and wine licenses. Some border on the petty or the trivial. Others are more glaring. The point is that despite the political scandals of the 1970s, Maryland's legislature still has not drawn the line on what is or isn't proper conduct.

Good Guy — Bad Guy

March 10, 1980

Remember the good guy-bad buy movies about youthful friends who find their lives pulling them in different directions — one as a priest, the other as a gangster? What makes these movies memorable is that real life is filled with such episodes. There's even one in the State House, though few are aware of it.

The good guy in this case is Julian L. Lapides, the whitest of white hats in the Maryland Senate. The bad guy is Paul E. Weisengoff, who proudly wears his black hat in the House of Delegates. As young men just out of college, they taught science together in the Baltimore County public schools. "Jack and I were good friends," recalled Mr. Weisengoff.

They're still on amicable terms, but they have followed conflicting paths politically.

Jack Lapides is a maverick liberal, from Baltimore's trendy central-city. He's forever pursuing lost causes, battling the powerful, raising issues others want ignored. He delights in tweaking Mayor Schaefer, denouncing the governor of the moment and setting off Senate pyrotechnics.

Paul Weisengoff, by contrast, is a loyal organization man who votes the interests of blue-collar, conservative South Baltimoreans. He's a supreme pragmatist, but also a supreme gameplayer. He has no peer in his ability to line up votes for a cause, no matter how dubious the merits.

Both have come a long way since their science-teaching days and now fill invaluable roles here. Just about every legislature has a Jack Lapides and a Paul Weisengoff, so it is instructive to look at their contributions.

It's been said of Paul Weisengoff that "he'd trade his grandmother in a deal." (This is an understatement. His Machiavellian mind also would have thought of a way to get his grandmother back.) He loves to wheel and deal, spending much time off the floor conferring with lawmakers and boasting.

Usually, he has the votes to back up these boasts. House Speaker Ben Cardin relies heavily on him to round up the votes. Mayor Schaefer is even more dependent on him. He's the one who can string together disparate voting blocs to pass controversial bills.

But mention his name to Common Cause and the reaction is (expletive deleted). Paul Weisengoff has done more than anyone to undermine government reformers. This year he is sabotaging revisions to the useless public campaign financing law (made useless by amendments he added in 1974). Nor is he popular with Governor Hughes. The two are feuding over control of harness racing in a game of political chicken likely to kill racing reform. And beyond this, he's working on a long-shot to bring jai alai to the city, for which he's been called a "Detroit mobster."

Paul Weisengoff jokes about his reputation as the legislature's villain. He is comfortable defending the effectiveness and practicality of Old Guard politics. His mission is to derail well-intentioned, but naive, "reform" measures.

He has done that more than once to Jack Lapides' bills, and more than once has been denounced for it by his ex-teaching colleague. But then, so has almost everyone else. Jack Lapides enjoys his role as the General Assembly's pain in the neck. He uses sharp words sure to provoke, like "venal," "despicable" and "outrageous." He promotes bills guaranteed to spark emotional debate — financial disclosure, euthanasia, ethics.

He is the Senate's conscience, reminding all what should be done, regardless of political consequences. He also is sometimes the last, stubborn holdout. His greatest moment came in 1972 when he threatened and then talked to death a race track consolidation bill that became an issue in the Mandel corruption trial.

At the moment, Jack Lapides is bewildered. He likes the current governor, and he's now co-chairman of the joint ethics committee. Yet Jack Lapides is never as happy as when he is on the losing side. So he is uneasy. "I get stomach cramps after every ethics meeting," he says. It's tougher implementing reform than slinging arrows from the Senate floor.

Jack Lapides can take comfort, though, that one legislator thinks he's doing a good job. "If I lived in his district, I'd vote for him," said conservative Old Guardsman Paul Weisengoff. "It may sound funny, but I think he's a good senator, even though I disagree with much of what he says."

It's enough to warm the heart of a hardened cynic. Come to think of it, it might make a good movie.

Jack Lapides, after retiring from the General Assembly in 1994 and losing a year later in a race for Baltimore City Comptroller, is practicing law in Baltimore. Paul Weisengoff is retired and living "Downey Ocean."

The Farmer and the Lawyer

March 24, 1980

When Governor Hughes wants to talk to "legislative leaders," he calls in the Senate president and the House speaker. These are the men selected by their colleagues to the preeminent posts in the General Assembly. Considerable prestige is attached to the jobs, plus an extra $4,000 above the $17,175 paid the other 186 legislators.

But these two men are far from equals, except at ceremonial functions such as bill-signings. The two current officeholders not only offer studies in contrasts, but reflect accurately the legislative bodies they represent.

Benjamin L. Cardin, 36, is a Baltimore lawyer and speaker of the House of Delegates. He is, without question, the most powerful man in the legislature. His influence among delegates is enormous, as is his popularity.

James Clark Jr., 61, is a Howard County dairy farmer and president of the Maryland Senate. Though he is almost universally well-liked by his fellow senators, Jim Clark carries little clout. He is not in Ben Cardin's league.

Ever since he was elected to the Assembly as a 23-year-old fresh out of Maryland Law School (first in his class), Ben Cardin has been a rising star. He has learned to master the quirks of the House, to play political games without sacrificing integrity. He comes from a prominent political family with strong liberal ties, but he knows when to take a stand and when prudence dictates a retreat. He also knows that nothing gets done in such a large body without compromise, and this often involves patching together fragile coalitions.

Much of his power stems from his reputation as the legislature's premier fiscal expert. Even though he is no longer chairman of the Ways and Means Committee, his expertise is so respected that any taxing measure coming out of the House bears the mark of Ben Cardin. And more likely than not, the House version prevails.

He runs the House with the same tight discipline he learned in his 14 years here from other speakers — John Hanson Briscoe, Thomas Hunter Lowe and Marvin Mandel. The 141-member House is an unwieldy body. For that reason, members submit to rigid rules that give the speaker the power to conduct business quickly and with a minimum of disruption.

Finding someone to say a bad word about Ben Cardin is difficult. He is extremely sensitive to minorities, be they Republicans, blacks or women. But when it's time to move bills through the House, the speaker can be a stern taskmaster, and the delegates recognize that.

Not so in the Senate, where the presiding officer is expected to be less a leader than an impartial referee, signaling the 46 players when it's time to serve, whether there has been a foot-fault and which shots are in play and which are not. Jim Clark models himself after William S. James, now the state treasurer, but for 12 years the Senate president, whose influence stemmed from an untarnished reputation for impartiality. Bill James was so fair with senators that when he put his prestige on the line, he won more often than not. Mr. James' successor, Steny Hoyer, tried to carve out a power base from the Senate presidency and ended up creating deep-seated bitterness that still is being felt. So Mr. Clark is content to stand on the rostrum as the independent-minded Senate meanders through its agenda on its own. This is a slow-paced chamber that talks endlessly before disposing of bills. It is very much like running a farm, and Jim Clark is happy doing both.

Jim Clark does not pretend to be an intellect, or a brilliant political tactician. He is a conservative, though he often votes with urban and liberal interests. He is a man of few words who believes in simply getting the job done. He clearly is comfortable with the Senate system, and has won high marks for running the Senate without providing strong direction.

This is a major difference between Jim Clark and Ben Cardin. Jim Clark does not have a burning ambition to change the world. He is content to let the legislative process run its course without interference. Ben Cardin takes a more active role, which could find him in a race for governor in 1982. He is a persuasive advocate for his causes. He tries to provide the lead for the rest of the legislature to follow. Sometimes, senators rebel at being pushed around by the House and its powerful speaker. But the way things work in Annapolis, they have little choice.

Jim Clark still runs his dairy farm outside Columbia, Md. Ben Cardin served as House speaker until 1986, when he was elected to Congress.

A Consummate Backstage Player

February 16, 1981

To those who work behind the scenes, a moment of stardom is a rare occasion. It happened once to Paul Cooper, the legislature's revered fiscal adviser, whose name was associated with the state's most farsighted and comprehensive tax-reform legislation, the Cooper-Hughes plan. That celebrity status, while firmly fixing his place in state history, cost Paul Cooper dearly in the years following passage of the tax-reform bill in 1967.

"Paul always regretted his prominence in the Cooper-Hughes plan," recalled Bill Ratchford, who succeeded Dr. Cooper as the General Assembly's chief financial consultant in 1974. "He felt it hurt his influence with the legislature afterward. His only advice to me when he retired was, 'Don't get out in front of an issue the way I did on Cooper-Hughes.'"

That is sound advice for backstage players, especially those dealing with the most important of government matters — budgets and taxes. Their role "is to advise and not to rule," says House Speaker Ben Cardin.

The fiscal adviser often comes in for criticism when his or her social and political values seem to coincide with the staff recommendations. Alice Rivlin, who assists Congress on budgetary matters, is under fire from Republicans on that very point. And some legislators here last week began wondering if their own budget analysts hadn't gone too far in determining the shape of this year's budget debate with little or no input from the senators and delegates.

Paul Cooper, who died eight days ago, rarely fell into that trap. "He was careful not to be intrusive," said Mr. Cardin. Though he held strong liberal views on such matters as education financing and tax reform, Dr. Cooper could be counted on to take even the most conservative of legislative ideas and devise a sound formula for it.

"There was not a governor or legislative leader who didn't go to Paul

Cooper to draft their bills, because they knew he would go ahead and do it — and improve it in the process," Mr. Cardin said. That, to the House speaker, is the mark of a good staff aide.

Yet it is doubtful if the Paul Cooper style could survive in this era's General Assembly. Gone are the powerful committee chairmen who made the big legislative decisions in backrooms. Gone is the intimacy of the smaller General Assembly in which everyone worked, ate and slept together. Gone is the opportunity to concentrate on just a handful of key issues. That is how Dr. Cooper operated. He could be found late at night drinking with legislative leaders at the Maryland Inn, arguing over issues as they made decisions on the spot. He developed tremendous influence. Some called him "Senator Cooper." Chairmen gave him the freedom to figure out how a program could be financed and then to draw up the bill. The integrity of his work was never challenged.

Today, though, legislators "would find that to be overstepping the bounds, going outside the role a bureaucrat should play," says John Hanson Briscoe, a former House speaker. "The younger people would resent it."

Not only that, but the legislature has gone Big Time. Dr. Cooper had a staff of 6; Mr. Ratchford has a staff of 139 and spends 80 percent of his days handling administrative chores. Thousands of bills now require the preparation of fiscal notes. Every item in the governor's $5.6 billion budget must be picked apart. In the post-Watergate legislature, requests for formulating even the most hopeless of spending bills must be honored. "It's not as much fun," Mr. Ratchford conceded. "Now it's all work and drudgery."

Dr. Cooper "would have been frustrated. He would have had a tough time dealing with today's legislature," said Mr. Cardin. It is a far more intricate and complex way of running government.

Some applaud the changes that have made the General Assembly more democratic — and more demanding of the backstage players. But has it meant better legislation? Paul Cooper may have consorted with legislators in ways that today's generation may find unacceptable. What came out in the end, though, were progressive, well-constructed laws that have stood the test of time. And after all, that's what we're after, isn't it?

Blair

March 2, 1981

Is this the land that time forgot, or do our eyes deceive us?

Isn't that Blair Lee III mingling with his Senate pals, testifying on finance bills, defending a university's budget request, partying at the Hilton bar? Didn't Blair Lee hang up his political cleats back in 1978 when Harry Hughes upset the acting governor in the Democratic primary?

We thought that the state's most aristocratic politician had retreated for good to his mansion in Montgomery County to clip bond coupons and attend to his beloved garden. We thought he had willed the Lee political fortunes to his son and namesake, Blair the fourth, who is known as B-4.

Well as Mark Twain would put it, reports of Blair Lee's political death have been greatly exaggerated. He may not be running for office, but he sure is keeping himself in shape. At least for a week, anyway.

"We usually go to Florida for the winter, but this year we couldn't afford it, so I'm coming to Annapolis for four days instead." This is how Blair Lee explained his unexpected State House appearance. Actually it was the result of his activity on the University of Maryland's board of regents (four days of budget hearings before two committees), his eagerness to testify on a package of spending-limit bills, a reunion dinner of past senators and an itch to see what's happening.

After all, Blair Lee has been beating a path to Annapolis since 1927, when he spent a week with his father, the House speaker (known simply as "the colonel") and ended up putting out a State House news sheet with a young journalist named Lou Azrael.

Blair appears slimmer and trimmer than when he was minding the government store in Marvin Mandel's lengthy absences. He still is an immaculate dresser, as befits one of his status. Fortunately, he has retained his flippancy, his relaxed demeanor, his stately use of the language. He is still a patrician with a sense of humor.

He still is direct and honest as well. What about the feud between the city and Montgomery County over school aid? "It's all the city's fault. For years we worked it out quietly behind the scenes. But then the city got greedy... and then they did that stupid thing of joining the court suit [to require equity in aid distribution]. That brought it out in the open, and the local papers picked it up and started screaming about it. Our officials had no choice but to react to it." What about the state's practically non-existent lieutenant governor, Sam Bogley? "It's a ridiculous situation. I don't know who is to blame... Marvin [Mandel] got a lot of mileage out of me. For ten years, I handled everything, and I mean everything, dealing with education. Marvin didn't have interest. Once, when the Lee Commission was formed [to devise a new aid formula] we had a number of correspondences back and forth from the commission to the governor... I would write one letter from the commission and then compose another in reply and rush across the hall to get Marvin's signature. It was a real game."

What about higher education? "We've got to do something about the situation in Baltimore. It's a real mess of colleges competing for turf. I would back anything that would be an improvement... I don't buy *The Sun's* line about how horrible it is for a poor child to have to travel all the way to College Park for a quality education. Why they're practically jumping at the chance to get away from home and momma."

Blair Lee was treated with enormous respect last week in Annapolis. Legislators and lobbyists and staffers listened as though an oracle were speaking. Later, they reflected on how much Blair Lee's presence is missed around the State House.

What is missed most is the sense of dedication he brought to government, a dedication that has been in his family since the American Revolution. He was rarely nasty or vindictive or shallow in his thinking. He utilized a sharp intellect to hammer out actions that fit the facts of life, Annapolis-style. He never took this high-pressured world too seriously. He was, above all, a totally civilized politician, something this town has not seen since he departed.

Blair Lee died on Oct. 26, 1985, at age 69.

Another Throttlebottom?

April 6, 1981

Samuel Walter Bogley III has a large, well-furnished office on the second floor of the State House. He has a small but loyal staff. He is conscientious and puts in a full workday. He is paid $52,500 a year. It is not for his skills and abilities that he is paid so well. Sam Bogley earns his money by being the voters' insurance policy. As lieutenant governor, his sole function is to be around should the governor die or be incapacitated. The state constitution sets out no functions for the lieutenant governor, and Harry Hughes has followed suit.

Part of Sam Bogley's problem is that he is always being compared with the only other lieutenant governor this state has had. Blair Lee III was actually a deputy governor. He shared the workload with Marvin Mandel, handled much of the tedious, but vital, budget detail, lobbied vigorously for administration bills, and assumed full command whenever the governor left the state. It was a hard act to follow.

Mr. Bogley suffers from a bigger difficulty, though: the governor lacks confidence in his nominal No. 2 man. Sam Bogley was a last-minute, desperation add-on to the Hughes ticket in 1978, and the governor has never forgotten that first blow-up over the abortion issue in early 1979. Mr. Bogley has not impressed Mr. Hughes with his brilliance or his political sophistication. The two men are civil, even like each other. But there is no partner relationship. Sam Bogley is left to sit in his office to do whatever strikes him.

This is a familiar political scenario. It has happened to most of our vice presidents and many of this country's lieutenant governors. It prompted the creation of a classic stereotype vice president in the Pulitzer Price-winning musical of the Thirties, "Of Thee I Sing." Alexander Throttlebottom was his name. He had no idea why he was vice president, what the office meant or what he was supposed to do. His redeeming characteristics were his basic decency and goodness.

The only way Throttlebottom could get into the White House was to take the public tour. At one point, the guide asked about the vice president:

> *Throttlebottom*: He's a nice fellow when you get to know him, but nobody wants to know him.
> *Guide*: What's the matter with him?
> *T*: There's nothing the matter with him. Just vice president.
> *G*: Well, what does he do all the time?
> *T*: He sits around in the parks, and feeds the pigeons, and takes walks, and goes to the movies. The other day, he was going to join the library, but he had to have two references, so he couldn't get in.
> *G*: But when does he do all his work?
> *T*: What work?

Maryland voters were told by politicians in 1970 there was a need for an elected lieutenant governor. So the voters complied. Now, the voters may be having second thoughts. Though Sam Bogley is hardly as pathetic a character as Alexander Throttlebottom, he contributes little to the Hughes government. He is extremely friendly and kind-hearted, sympathetic legislators and administration officials say, but...

In other states, the lieutenant governor fills a variety of roles, from presiding over the state Senate, to heading state commissions and agencies, to acting as the governor's representative on panels. There are a wealth of substantive assignments that might be given to Mr. Bogley. They won't, though.

With Mr. Bogley continuing to look like a one-term lieutenant governor, it might be a good time to reflect on what went wrong. Should the largely ceremonial office of secretary of state be abolished and the duties turned over to the lieutenant governor? Should the legislature be allowed to assign specific duties to the lieutenant governor? What about putting the lieutenant governor on gubernatorial commissions and task forces?

I would cast my vote for getting rid of the secretary of state, and allowing the legislature to put the lieutenant governor on any board or commission as an ex-officio member. We have now seen in just one decade the two extremes governors can take toward their ticketmates. If we don't want a Throttlebottom situation, some big changes will have to be made.

Sam Bogley, after serving one term as lieutenant governor, disappeared from statewide politics. He practices law in Prince George's County.

Marvin, What Do We Do Now?

January 25, 1982

There is a moment of arresting insight in the Robert Redford film, "The Candidate." It happens at the end of the film just after the Redford character, a naive, first-time political candidate with a pretty face and a famous father, wins election to the United States Senate through a slick, media-public relations campaign. The winner pulls his campaign manager into an empty room, looks at him with an expression of fear and bewilderment, and says, "Marvin, what do we do now?"

In football you can always punt. But in politics, you're stuck with the ball until your term runs out.

What do you do after the cheering has stopped?

In Jimmy Carter's case, that problem came to dominate his entire four years as president.

Hamilton Jordan had devised a masterful strategy for capturing the presidency for Mr. Carter: Jimmy Carter was to be the virtuous outsider who would kick "them" out of Washington and get things cleaned up. But once the goal of winning was attained, the new president never was able to govern effectively.

What might be called the Jimmy Carter syndrome also has dogged Maryland's present governnor, Harry Hughes.

Elected on a one-issue platform — restoring integrity to the Maryland government — Mr. Hughes has had trouble ever since conveying his vision and purpose, setting goals and achieving them.

Just as Mr. Carter has never seemed capable of adapting to Washington-style politics, especially as played by the Congress, Governor Hughes has had enormous difficulty figuring out how to establish a viable relationship with the state legislature.

He has spent three years stubbing his toes during the annual meeting of

the General Assembly. This is especially surprising, since Harry Hughes is no neophyte: He spent the Sixties and Seventies as state senator, majority leader and transportation secretary.

It is not for lack of sincerity that Mr. Hughes has floundered. Nor is it a case of incompetence. The governor has put together some outstanding programs, has operated a "clean" government and has done it all without raising his voice in anger. He also has finally assembled a capable staff. Yet some ingredient is missing.

The governor's relationship with the legislature is strained. This was obvious from the tepid reception he was given before and after his state-of-the-state address last week. The "standing ovation" from lawmakers was an obligatory gesture undertaken without enthusiasm. Not once did they break into applause during his well-delivered, forceful speech.

In recent weeks, the governor has become increasingly critical of some legislators for thwarting his programs and for their criticism of him.

He has complained — gently, but often — that the press has ignored his accomplishments and has harped on minor flubs. He says he will have to go to the voters directly to get his message across.

That sounds like a political campaigner talking.

While this may be good campaign strategy, it will not eliminate the problem.

The reality is that the Hughes administration has yet to prove it can get along with the legislature.

It keeps losing many of the key battles through lack of attention to detail, lack of follow-through, a failure to attend to the diplomatic niceties of politics and a failure to seize the initiative and turn it to the governor's advantage.

Fortunately for Harry Hughes, his political future does not appear threatened. His own polls show him far ahead of any challenger.

In fact, his biggest challenge may occur before his campaign even gets under way, as he tries for a fourth time to master the legislative part of his job.

Fair Joe Curran

March 15, 1982

For someone who has been in the Maryland General Assembly for nearly a quarter-century, Joe Curran hasn't accumulated much influence. By all odds, he should have by now.

Heir to one of Baltimore's strongest political organizations and possessing a name that guarantees his re-election, J. Joseph Curran Jr. has been chairman of the Senate Judicial Proceedings Committee for 16 years — twice the seniority of any other Senate chairman. His panel handles crucial, controversial issues, such as gun control, drinking age and divorce reforms. His counterpart in the House, Joseph E. Owens of Montgomery County, by imposing an almost military discipline and loyalty on his committee, has amassed enormous influence over the fate of bills. He has become a heavyweight in the legislative arena. Not so Joe Curran.

He is low-keyed, undemanding, noncommittal. He has no burning ambitions, no long-range political goals. He has cared deeply about certain issues over the years — the Vietnam war, gun control, abortions — but he has never been a forceful proponent, rather a patient explainer.

Mr. Curran takes an academic approach to the legislature. He loves the law and dotes on every change that is being made in it. He gets so involved in sorting out the subtle shadings in the issues that he often seems to lose track of political realities.

At the same time, it is difficult to find anyone in Annapolis who has anything mean to say about him. He is decent and sincere, someone who stands by his convictions. You'll never catch him criticizing another politician. Nor will he ever disparage an opposing idea without agonizing over the pros and cons at great length. Watching him give his committee reports on the Senate floor is a little like watching Hamlet. He has a nickname among legislative staffers and followers: "Fair Joe."

Mr. Curran has been in the General Assembly since 1958; he's been in the Senate since 1962. He took over the Judicial Proceedings Committee in 1967 during a palace revolt by liberals in which the Eastern Shore's tyrannical Frederick C. Malkus was stripped of his chairmanship. He seemed marked for bigger things, and it almost happened in 1968, when Mr. Curran, as an anti-Vietnam war candidate, took on incumbent U.S. Representative George Fallon and came within 985 votes of beating him. Some say he would have won that year had he campaigned a little harder. And he almost certainly could have won two years later had he relinquished his legislative seat to try again.

He didn't and Paul Sarbanes did. Now Mr. Sarbanes is a U.S. senator, and Mr. Curran is still in the state Senate.

Although he ran for Congress once more in 1976, Mr. Curran admits he did not have his heart in it. Some attribute that to the loss of a young son, a loss they say he never has gotten over. Whatever the reason, Joe Curran seems content to remain where he is. And at age 50, he is young enough that he could still be in the Senate when the next century arrives.

Clearly, though, politics is not an all-consuming passion for him. When the legislature is out of session, Mr. Curran works six days a week, mainly on his law practice; during the session, his work-week consists of seven days. In his 24 years in Annapolis, Mr. Curran has stayed overnight in Annapolis only 10 times, which must be something of a record. He insists on spending time with his family. He ignores the lobbyists who swarm around committee chairmen offering free meals, drinks, favors and advice. Instead, he limits his appearances to the two big lobbying dinners put on by the agriculture and seafood interests.

When he was asked last week about his future plans, Mr. Curran looked genuinely puzzled. "That's a good question," he said. Was he getting tired of the grueling legislative routine after 24 years? Yes. Had he lost some of his enthusiasm? Yes. But he will run again this fall, he said. After that? "I guess I'll just see what happens." Joe Curran is not about to be pushed into any hasty decisions.

Governor Hughes picked Joe Curran as his lieutenant governor in 1982. Mr. Curran was elected attorney general four years later.

No (Bill)s Allowed

May 25, 1982

Willard Morris is mellowing. That's not to say he is *mellow*. Far from it. He can still let loose with a harangue against the "plague of women vultures" (translation: the League of Women Voters). But his irascibility quotient isn't what it used to be. He's become a more cuddly, grandfatherly curmudgeon. Sort of a Scrooge in government clothing.

This could be Willard Morris' swan song, his last hurrah. He's been running the state's elections board since the office was set up to bring some order to the confusing array of 24 independent local boards all going their own way. That was 12 years ago. Willard Morris was appointed by Marvin Mandel back then, but he's managed to stay on the good side of Harry Hughes, too. Next year, Mr. Morris will be 70, and he almost definitely will be ready to retire to Silver Spring.

Willard Morris has become Maryland's election-law authority. He was instrumental in the 1960s in revising the state's election laws. Since then, he has implemented them. He's a walking encyclopedia on the subject. A constant stream of telephone calls and visitors pour into his office in election years, seeking the answers to the minutiae of filing for office, filling out campaign finance documents, registering to vote and drawing up the ballots.

At the moment, it is the July 6 filing deadline that concerns Mr. Morris. There could be 3,000 candidates running for elected offices across the state, for every post from local sheriff to governor and senator. That means lots of confusion, lots of questions. The Court of Appeals' foot-dragging in setting the final boundary lines for the state legislative races has not helped. It gives Mr. Morris more to worry about and Mr. Morris is a constant worrier to begin with.

Willard Morris is what some would call an old-school pol. He became active in Silver Spring civic groups, then ran a number of political races with his friend, Blair Lee III. The two became so successful they were laughingly called the "bosses of good government" in Montgomery County. After running the county's elections board, Mr. Morris moved up to his present post at the same time Blair Lee joined the new Mandel administration as secretary of state. Politicians usually stay on their best behavior around Mr. Morris. With good reason. When a political candidate gets in a bind over some obscure provision of state election law, a friendly Willard Morris has been known to find a loophole to paper over the problem. But if you cross him, his strict interpretation can be unyielding.

Take the matter of Francis B. (as in Bill) Burch, the longtime attorney general who filed for governor in 1978. Mr. Burch wanted to be listed on the ballot as Francis (Bill) Burch. It sounded chummier, less foreboding. The then-attorney general even went into court so that he became, legally, Francis (Bill) Burch. But he never checked with Willard Morris.

That was a fatal breach of etiquette. (Bill) is a nickname, the elections-board chief declared angrily. And nicknames are forbidden by law. There will be no (Bill) on the ballot, he ordered.

Mr. Burch wouldn't back down. He appealed to the courts. But he never got Willard Morris's no-(Bill)s-allowed decision overturned. He decided to drop out of the race instead, and became a private citizen, a position that doesn't require asking Willard Morris for permission to be called (Bill).

That should serve as a warning for political newcomers who must cross paths with Willard Morris this summer. The elections-board administrator may have mellowed a tad, but it still pays to watch your manners.

Willard A. Morris died on April 29, 1994, at age 81.

The Harry Hughes Enigma

March 28, 1983

The Harry Hughes enigma continues. It is hard to believe that the same Harry Hughes who proved so successful with the 1982 General Assembly is now taking his lumps in 1983. Some maintain he is being clobbered. What had been billed in the past as the "new" Harry Hughes now looks more like the older, less effective version.

To say this talk about ineffectiveness irritates the governor and his staff is putting it mildly Recent press accounts of the governor's fumbling of his legislative chores have raised hackles in State House executive suites. The press, the Hughes staffers concluded, just doesn't understand.

Well, does it? This is an intriguing question. Is this heavy criticism the creation of a State House press corps bored by a dreary legislature and a governor who avoids controversies and shuns the limelight?

There is no doubt that in the eyes of journalists, Mr. Hughes suffers in comparison with his predecessor, Marvin Mandel, who was activist, effective and controversial. It is also a fact that Mr. Hughes' actions (and non-actions) are carefully scrutinized by the press for any signs of strength or weakness, for signs of how well he plays the game.

In the House and Senate, the perception of the governor differs markedly from the view in the executive suites. That difference is what the reporters are reflecting in their articles. Few legislators look to the governor for the kind of direction and leadership traditionally associated with chief executives. While they admire Mr. Hughes, he doesn't inspire them.

"I really like the guy," said one influential senator. "He's so honest and sincere. But it's hard to go to the wall for him. He's got that laid-back style and he's apolitical. You know there's no reward in it for you and that he's likely to leave you hanging"

A prime example is the pension-reform measure. A massive lobbying

campaign was waged by state employee unions and teachers to kill the bill. But Senate President Melvin Steinberg persuaded the Senate to go along with his reform measure despite the enormous pressures. It passed the Senate, only to die in the House. Meanwhile, the governor, who had at one point endorsed taking action now, backed off, urging yet another study.

"What a golden opportunity Hughes had," said the senator, "We're in the first year of our four-year terms. Nobody's worried about getting reelected. And the bill has already cleared the Senate. The governor should have done something. He could have passed it, if he had tried. The Sunshine Soldiers in the Senate [who backed the pension bill] took the heat from everyone on this. Next year, they'll try to get back in the good graces of state workers and teachers. Then what is Hughes going to do?"

When he is sufficiently motivated, Mr. Hughes can be a persuasive executive. But his staff does not seem to stay abreast of legislative twists and turns, of sudden mood swings that can doom bills. Nor are his aides good at winning converts. That leaves Mr. Hughes as chief persuader and lobbyist. This is a heavy burden, especially for a shy man who believes in maintaining a separation between executive and legislative branches.

There is still time in the next two weeks for Mr. Hughes to salvage key parts of his legislative package. Were that to happen, the verdict on the governor's performance would change. If that doesn't happen, there will be more press accounts about the failure of leadership from the executive. Like it or not, people in Maryland (including legislators and reporters) look to the governor for direction. They expect strong action. Yet this is not the incumbent governor's style.

Harry Hughes is far from a recluse. His days are filled with meetings with staffers, with interest groups and most often with legislators this time of year. And spurred by recent press criticism of his work (or lack of hard work) this session, he has intensified his outreach mission to lawmakers. Still, he has a lot of catching up do. It already is too late for some administration bills. And based on his off-again, on-again performance of past years, there is no telling how successful Mr. Hughes will be.

Teachers Overdid It

April 9, 1984

Today may be the last official day of this year's General Assembly session, but it hardly represents the legislative climax. This is the denouement, the windup of the play, when loose ends are tied together before the curtain falls and the audience goes home. In the space of 15 hours, hundreds of bills will be enacted as the House and Senate accelerate the legislative process before that midnight *sine die* adjournment.

This fast finish may be exciting to watch but it is lousy democracy. So many bills are being voted on in two chambers that no one has a chance to examine them all. It is time to keep an eye out for "snakes" and "bell-ringers," bills that reek of special interest and financial windfalls.

Looking back on the 90-day legislative session, there is no question when the action reached its zenith: The pension-reform/education-aid votes. Everything hinged on the outcome of these tallies. Even Governor Hughes' repeated fumbling of the state budget — he never did come up with an acceptable plan to balance revenues and expenses — receded in significance next to the fight over these two key bills.

Repercussions from the pension/education struggles, so intricately intertwined, will linger. No one emerged from the battle unscathed.

The biggest losers may have been the Maryland State Teachers Association and its local counterparts. They waged the most intensive — some would say excessive — lobbying campaign in years. They invoked an "end-of-the-world" crusade, as though survival of the teaching profession were at stake. They tried to intimidate legislators through sheer bulk: Letters so voluminous they couldn't be answered; protesters so numerous they overflowed the State House grounds; phone calls so constant lawmakers complained of harassment.

Still, it was not enough. So pickets appeared on the front lawn of one legislator's home; one delegate lost his $60,000-a-year job for voting in favor of pension reform; many other delegates were harshly threatened that a vote against the teachers would mean the end of their political careers. "Our pensions are being cut," was the cry often heard. That's what the teachers seemed to believe. The fact that this was a misstatement (no existing benefits are being cut; only future cost-of-living pension allowances are being limited) did not faze the determined lobbyists. Nor did it bother them that many teachers and state workers will make out better under pension reform. That information was never disseminated to the rank and file.

When their strategy backfired, just barely, in the House, the teachers' unions turned their wrath on House Speaker Benjamin Cardin, Senate President Melvin Steinberg and this newspaper. Rather then looking at the real source of the problem — their lobbying tactics infuriated even supporters — they pointed an accusing finger elsewhere. And vowed vengeance.

That is not going to win the teachers new friends in the State House. Some longtime Annapolis observers believe the credibility and clout of the teachers' unions have been badly damaged. Good will and civil disagreement are hallmarks of the legislative debate in Maryland. Groups that step over the line lose leverage — sometimes for years.

One other aspect of the pension/education battles is worth noting. The ineptness of city legislators on the education-aid bill, especially in the Senate, was an embarrassment to Mayor Schaefer. It underlined the danger the city faces when Baltimore's Ben Cardin is no longer speaker. His immense power saved the city from losing school aid this year. But he won't be speaker after 1986. If the city's pressing needs are to be met in Annapolis, it will take a governor willing to flex his muscles for Baltimore. Could it be that Don Schaefer is beginning to see the value of running for governor himself?

An Elder Statesman Looks Ahead

February 14, 1985

At the age of 10 he could neither read nor write. He didn't graduate from high school until he was 21. He was 28 when he received his B.A. degree and 44 when he earned his master's. He didn't become a politician until he was 49. Now Clarence W. Blount is majority leader of the Maryland Senate, vice chairman of the powerful Budget and Taxation Committee, chairman of one of the two budget subcommittees and one of the senior members of the Senate, with 15 years of service.

It was a long trip from the tobacco fields of Beaufort County, North Carolina, to the streets of Baltimore, and even a longer journey to the legislative halls of Annapolis for Mr. Blount. Yet at an age when most people are thinking about collecting their Social Security benefits (he'll be 64 in April), Mr. Blount could be on the verge of achieving political preeminence in Baltimore City.

How does Congressman Blount sound? Or Mayor Blount? These are not pipe dreams. Clarence Blount could well emerge in the next year or two as a compromise choice for one of these two offices.

That might shock some of Mr. Blount's colleagues. He is not, after all, quick on his feet, a riveting speaker or a consummate political operator. He does not have Benjamin Cardin's legislative acumen, Melvin Steinberg's political chutzpah, Harry Hughes' telegenic presence or William Donald Schaefer's flamboyant boosterism.

"I know my limitations," Mr. Blount said recently. He is, essentially, a plodder. He lacks the overriding ambition that so many politicians possess. But there is a human quality, a warmth, a caring for people that comes across as genuine and intense.

Had he wanted, Mr. Blount now could be chairman of Budget and Taxation, the General Assembly's most potent committee. He turned down

Senate President Steinberg's offer and accepted the vice chairmanship, in spite of intense pressure from Mayor Schaefer.

"I didn't need the ego gratification" he said. And he feared that taking the chairmanship would anger a key Baltimore City ally on the panel, Senator Laurence Levitan of Montgomery County. Mr. Blount's decision has turned out to be a wise one. He remains in a strong position to help city-related programs and to influence votes in committee. At the same time, Chairman Levitan and Mr. Blount have developed a good working relationship that has benefited the city.

Mr. Blount is an elder stateman in the legislature's increasingly influential black caucus. He has become for many of them an example, a successful educator-turned-politician. When the caucus was split into factions a few years ago, the members turned to Mr. Blount. His tenure as chairman of the caucus served to smooth over some of the dissension and gave the group a new sense of direction.

His legislative district in Northwest Baltimore contains most of the city's well-to-do black communities. Yet he has also headed the Community Action Agency in the city for 16 years, overseeing the disbursement of poverty-program funds and thwarting efforts to radicalize the agency. Over the years he has won the trust and backing of most of his district's influential business and political leaders, both black and white.

It is this broad-based appeal that could make Mr. Blount a figure to watch in the next two years. He worries about what would happen if a divisive black candidate were to become mayor. The shock waves that might hit the city's white business community and some of its white residents could be devastating, he believes.

Likewise, Mr. Blount feels the city cannot afford to be represented in Congress by someone who either isn't up to the job or frightens many Baltimore residents and businessmen. When Representative Parren J. Mitchell retires from his Seventh District seat next year, a free-for-all is expected. Unless a consensus candidate emerges, Mr. Blount might decide to step forward.

"Baltimore has been very good to me," said the Senate majority leader. He is an inveterate booster for the city and he speaks out on the problems of blacks, without the Schaefer flair and without Congressman Mitchell's anger. He doesn't want to do anything that would jeopardize the city's economic renewal or antagonize groups that might be helpful some day. Clarence Blount's brand of politics could prove popular with Baltimore's mayoral or congressional voters — if he decides to take the plunge.

Clarence Blount is running this year for his eighth term in the state Senate.

Insider's Insider

August 1, 1985

The term "Hocker rocker" hasn't been heard for almost 20 years, which explains why the death of George Hocker last weekend stirred so little interest. That is unfortunate. George Hocker merited considerably more attention than the routine obituary stories he received. For eight years, 1958 - 1966, Mr. Hocker was the second-most powerful man in political Maryland. Some would argue that his influence at times exceeded that of his close friend and patron, Gov. J. Millard Tawes. "Hockerism" became an issue in many political campaigns of the 1960s.

Mr. Hocker never held elective or appointive office. He was a "kitchen cabinet" variety of political adviser, a looming unofficial presence who helped plan Governor Tawes' actions and line up the votes to see that the governor would have his way with the legislature.

He could be intimidating, but he also could be genial. His obsession was the success of the Tawes administration.

A "Hocker rocker" was a device used by anti-Tawes legislators as a bargaining chip with Mr. Hocker, who was the longtime lobbyist for local brewers. Any attempt to raise Maryland's ridiculously low beer tax would send Mr. Hocker rocking back on his heels, ready to negotiate a deal with the legislators. In the end, the beer tax increase always failed and legislators came away with a few more Green Bag appointments or some other slight accommodation.

It would be a mistake to write off Mr. Hocker and the "Hocker rocker" as ancient history. His influence on the political life of this state is still being felt today. And his style of behind-the-scenes politics could soon reappear in the governor's office.

Mr. Hocker, operating out of Democratic headquarters at the old Emerson Hotel, set a new standard for political fund-raising. In his hands, the $100-a-plate dinner became almost an art form. Anyone who depended on state business was expected to buy his share of dinners — perhaps even a full table. The notion of putting the heat on state businessmen to buy expensive tickets to dinners for the politically powerful didn't originate with Marvin Mandel's mentor, Irvin Kovens.

Nor did Kovens and Company originate the idea of funneling insurance business on state jobs to a new firm with special ties to the governor. That was Mr. Hocker's innovation.

He helped set up Tidewater Insurance Company in 1958, shortly before Millard Tawes took the oath of office as governor. By the time Mr. Tawes was preparing for retirement eight years later, Tidewater had become the third-largest insurance firm in Maryland. It was known as the political insurance company.

When the Tawes era ended, so did Mr. Hocker's power. His enemies got their revenge. Mr. Hocker's much-cherished desire to serve on the University of Maryland board of regents was rejected by the State Senate, 21-20, only days before Millard Tawes left office. Mr. Hocker was forced out of Tidewater Insurance by W. Dale Hess and the Rodgers brothers in 1971, and the Mandel-Kovens alliance pushed through a tripling of the beer tax a few years later.

But when Millard Tawes was governor, George Hocker wielded immense power. Few dared to cross him.

The staples of deal-making back then were patronage appointments and campaign funds for local ward-heelers.

Today, the Green Bag is so slim that few politicians can be influenced in that way; most of the choice appointed jobs have been put in the merit system. And "walkaround" money is not what it used to be; candidates in the 1980s prefer to use campaign funds for television advertising, not for handouts to political clubs. So deals must be struck over legislative issues — usually trades involving administration bills and parochial projects sought by legislative factions.

But the need for a fundraiser, head-knocker and legislative conductor has not changed. Harry Hughes' rocky relations with the General Assembly stem in part from his refusal to appoint someone as his latter-day Hocker. The next governor could change all that, bringing to the State House a new era of powerful gubernatorial insiders.

Chapter 2

Crisis
at the S&Ls

S&L Lies and Deceptions

May 23, 1985

The entire system of banking and savings in America is based upon a false premise that there's enough money in the bank or savings and loan association to pay off every customer who wants his money back. It doesn't work that way.

Yet we pretend this is the case. We give our money to the financial institutions. They invest it and pay us interest for the privilege of using our money to make money for them. But if all the depositors asked for all their money tomorrow, the banks and S&Ls couldn't comply. That's known as a liquidity crisis. And as we are discovering, it also is an asset crisis for the worst-run institutions.

Most bankers and thrift officials invest our money prudently. But some of them risk our money on more speculative ventures. There are rules to prevent S&Ls from plunging too deeply into land deals and office buildings. S&Ls are supposed to be providing home mortgages, after all. It now turns out that too many of them were not holding onto enough capital in case of an emergency — and no one was enforcing the rules.

To qualify for federal insurance, banks are supposed to maintain a net worth (assets minus liabilities) of roughly 6.6 percent. They also must set aside considerable funds in case of bad loans.

In contrast, Maryland's S&Ls don't have any requirement for keeping a "loan-loss reserve." Many of the 102 thrifts caught up in the present crisis can't meet even the minimum 5 percent net worth needed to qualify for federal savings and loan insurance.

Once problems cropped up in Maryland, officials in the S&L industry concocted an elaborate series of lies to make it seem as if there were plenty of money available to handle a run on their institutions. It was a bluff.

For 23 years, S&L officials have advertised that they are insured up

to $100,000 per account by something called the Maryland Savings-Share Insurance Corporation. It sounds official, like an agency of the government. Its emblem even resembles the official Maryland state seal. "Your money is secure," the S&Ls told the public.

The truth is that MSSIC was little more than a glorified self-insurance fund for the industry. It was run by the S&Ls, not the state. The fund's directors and officials cared more about promoting the industry than in policing it. So when troubles were uncovered at two big S&Ls, the reaction of MSSIC officials was to cover up, to mislead the public and the government.

The worse the situation may have looked from the inside, the harder MSSIC officers tried to paint a rosy picture. They feared what would happen if the public were told the truth.

Sir Walter Scott hit it on the mark: "Oh, what a tangled web we weave, when first we practice to deceive!" Once that web of S&L deceptions and lies is unraveled, there will be a harsh day of reckoning.

During Maryland's earlier savings and loan scandal, in the late 1950s and early 1960s, the government was more clearly at fault. There was no regulation of any phase of the S&L industry.

It was easy for out-of-state crooks to link up with local politicians to defraud the public. Plunk down $30 for a license, open a post box address, pick a name such as "Federated Swiss Insurance Underwriters of Tangier, Morocco" and let the S&Ls advertise that deposits are fully protected.

The fact that these were shell corporations never was revealed until the S&Ls started to collapse and depositors lost millions.

Back then, Governor Hughes was in the state Senate, Attorney General Stephen Sachs was an assistant U.S. attorney who helped prosecute those involved in the scandal, and Louis L. Goldstein was in his first term as the state comptroller. These men were in position to see clearly what happened to Maryland's S&Ls.

This time it was no secret that certain S&Ls were being run recklessly. Yet government and industry leaders did nothing to curb their activities. One thrift official told legislators last week that he and his colleagues referred to officers at these S&Ls as "the Baltimore crazies." But rather than jar public confidence in the industry, S&L leaders chose to remain silent.

Nor did they demand in private that these high-flyers be stopped before they wrecked the entire system. When an industry is in the position of policing itself, there must be tough crackdowns on abusers. That didn't happen among Maryland's savings and loans, and now all of the S&Ls are paying the price for it. It is turning out to be a tragically high price.

Hughes Ho-Hums a Smoking Gun

October 31, 1985

Harry Hughes now is trying to explain away the so-called "smoking gun" memo of the savings and loan controversy.

Written last year by a consultant to the governor, the memo warned of "very serious problems" in the savings and loan industry.

The warning went unheeded, and the governor is denying any specific knowledge of an S&L crisis until May 2 of this year.

Mr. Hughes is playing with semantics. He might not have received a "line-by-line item" briefing on S&L irregularities until five months ago, but he certainly had reason for concern well before then.

"At no time did anyone bring this to my attention as a crisis," the governor now says.

The memo he received from consultant George W. Liebmann a year ago this month didn't sound "enough of an alarm."

The governor is right. Sirens were not set off by the Liebmann memorandum. No one called the S&L situation a "crisis." A perceptive person, though, could not miss the dangers cited by Mr. Liebmann.

Ejner Johnson didn't miss it. The governor's chief of staff forwarded the Liebmann memo to the administration's regulatory secretary, Frederick Dewberry, and the governor's staff lawyer, Benjamin Bialek, with a cover letter noting that the memo "raises some particularly troubling problems" pertaining to self-dealing by S&L officials and the solvency of the private S&L insurance fund.

He suggested that these officials meet with Mr. Liebmann to obtain specifics, since the points outlined "call for more immediate solutions to regulatory problems."

The bureaucracy's response was what the governor called a "ho-hum" letter from Charles Brown, director of the Division of Savings and Loan

Associations, the agency that regulated S&Ls. In his letter, Mr. Brown defended the state's S&L system. Yet the director also expressed considerable agreement with some of Mr. Liebmann's conclusions.

"I, too, have some reservations about insider loans and have often felt this should be more restrictive," Mr. Brown wrote. "As a matter of fact, I have often felt this should be prohibited altogether, especially insofar as commercial lending, land acquisition and development loans, etc., are concerned."

He said the state could well be pressured to back the S&L deposits with taxpayers' dollars in the event of a run.

Still no alarm bells, no gongs being rung outside the governor's mansion. No one was using the term "crisis."

Instead, there was the governor's paid consultant warning Mr. Hughes of S&L troubles in a memo on October 5, 1984.

There was the governor's chief of staff expressing concern about "troubling problems" in the S&L industry on October 30, 1984.

And in a letter November 21, 1984, there was the director of the S&L regulatory agency noting his "reservations" about certain S&L practices that he felt should be outlawed.

Why, then, didn't Mr. Hughes pursue this matter in November and December of last year?

Why wasn't additional legislation prepared to deal with the problem in January, February or March?

Why was the issue dropped after Mr. Brown's response?

The Hughes administration does not anticipate problems well. It is not aggressive in solving problems early. But if there is an emergency, the Hughes team can handle it.

So the key word is "crisis."

Had that one word been used by Mr. Liebmann in his memo, the Hughes administration might have reacted sooner.

It does, after all, come down to a matter of semantics — and knowing how to sound an alarm that Mr. Hughes can hear.

George Liebmann continues to practice law in Baltimore and ran as a Republican for the U.S. Senate in 1998.

Harry Hughes as Harry Truman

January 16, 1986

A reshaped, restyled Harry Hughes rolled off his media advisers' assembly line last week to a decidedly mixed reception. The new Hughes model is noisier and has more visibility, but critics were quick to notice that underneath the hood there weren't many changes.

This refurbished image is part of a Hughes campaign theme that harks back to the Truman upset of 1948 and the now-famous war cry, "Give 'em hell, Harry!"

The governor, who spent three months in self-imposed silence due to the savings and loan debacle, re-emerged forcefully: A special television address to the citizens of Maryland; a speech to a joint session of the General Assembly announcing his S&L bailout plan; his first press conference since October; a local television news interview; a local radio interview, and yesterday's budget and state-of-the-state address.

His rhetoric was defiant and warlike:

"We are winning the fight against the corruption and greed of a few high-rollers."

"This crisis happened on my watch... The buck really stops here."

"I have kept silent even when it hurt."

"[If necessary] I will fight alone on the course I'm committed to."

"I will fight against any action to bail out the depositor at the expense of the taxpayer."

"We've got to draw the line, and no amount of pressure should move us to step over that line."

You can almost hear Clint Eastwood mumbling: "Go ahead, make my day." It is the image of the tough but sincere Western lawman preparing for a showdown.

In this case, it is Governor Hughes standing tall against the potshots of his enemies.

Listen to Mr. Hughes' concluding words in his special address to the legislature last week. When future generations look back, Mr. Hughes said, "I will be known as the governor who saved the depositor, who spared the taxpayer, and who against all odds and all intimidation stood tall, stood firm and delivered for Maryland."

It is Gary Cooper defending the town against the bad guys and then riding off with Grace Kelly in "High Noon." It is Alan Ladd in "Shane."

It is John Wayne at his finest.

But most of all, it is Harry Truman battling for his political life, "against all odds and all intimidation," to win the presidency.

Mr. Hughes has decided he will not retire meekly. He and his aides believe they have gotten a raw deal, and the governor is taking the brunt of the public's S&L wrath unfairly. And they see their political enemies — what could be termed the Mandel-Schaefer coalition — behind much of the agitation.

Given Mr. Hughes' sinking political popularity, a "give'em hell" approach makes sense. But there are problems that any Hughes-for-Senator strategy might not be able to overcome:

• The governor is late starting his comeback. Three solid months of growing anti-Hughes sentiment will be tough to counter.

• Though Mr. Hughes would like to put the S&L crisis behind him, he has no control over events. For instance, his first-week media blitz was overshadowed by release of the Preston report, the Jeffrey Levitt indictment and the Levitts' contempt sentencing. Savings and loan issues — rewriting state financial regulations, the Hughes bailout plan — will dominate most of the General Assembly session. New indictments and trials in the spring and summer will keep the public focused on S&Ls.

• Mr. Hughes is caught between angry depositors who won't forgive him for withholding their money and taxpayers who won't forgive him for using state funds to bail out the thrift customers.

• None of the other Democratic candidates for the Senate are tainted by the S&L crisis. Representatives Barbara Mikulski and Michael Barnes are popular in their congressional districts and are regarded as effective, aggressive legislators. Baltimore County Executive Donald Hutchinson has broad appeal in his county and a solid record of executive leadership. By contrast, the governor emerges from the S&L imbroglio looking unpopular, ineffective and indecisive.

Mr. Hughes proved in 1978 that he does not bow out of political races because his fortunes seem dim. In the eight months before primary election day, strange things can happen. That's what the governor is counting on. It would be a comeback to rival the upset pulled off by that other Harry.

Birthday of a Monster

May 8, 1986

It could be called "The Monster That Wouldn't Die." One year after the runs on Maryland savings and loans began, the issue refuses to go away. Every time it seems matters are about to be resolved, a new aspect of the problem pops up. Four months ago tomorrow, Governor Harry Hughes went on Baltimore and Washington television to announce his plan for ending the S&L crisis. He said the sale of two troubled S&Ls was imminent and promised a long-anticipated repayment program for Old Court S&L depositors. None of it has happened yet. Key parts may fall into place in a week or so, but at least one S&L sale remains in limbo as federal regulators worry about the competency of the proposed suitor.

The S&L monster won't vanish.

Ask Attorney General Stephen Sachs. We are still awaiting his long-promised indictments of S&L figures. Meanwhile, Mr. Sachs has been forced to defend himself against new charges that he was told about the S&L crisis way before it happened — and didn't act. It is tough to campaign for governor with the S&L monster still about.

Mr. Hughes must feel that way, too. Only in his case, he's trying to run for U.S. Senator. Mr. Hughes remains stuck in controversies over the Old Court depositor payment plan, the soon-to-be concluded sale of Community S&L, the not-yet-approved sale of First Maryland and the likely liquidation of Ridgeway S&L. And if there are charges lodged against former savings-regulatory officials, the question of Mr. Hughes' failure to stop the crisis before it started could surface again.

This has been a nightmarish 12 months for the governor. It began, publicly at least, a year ago today when management changes at Old Court were quietly announced. The one-column, front-page *Sun* story the next morning was headlined, "Old Court reveals problems." The article was cautiously worded, but it was enough to start a run. Bit by bit the depth of the thrifts' negligence and insolvency came out. And the lines outside the S&Ls, not surprisingly, grew longer.

The governor, meanwhile, was in Israel, a trip that in hindsight was a terrible blunder. He knew a major crisis was brewing when he left on May 4. But it was a behind-closed-doors crisis. Officials still felt they could handle the situation without informing the public. Canceling the Israel trip would only alarm people, the governor was advised.

Yet by that time, a "silent run" on the high-roller thrifts by big investors was in full swing — withdrawals spiraled over $400 million. There was no way to keep Maryland's thrifts from sinking, and certainly no way to keep it quiet. Then Mr. Hughes compounded the problem by failing to return home promptly as the lines spread to more thrifts. He wavered, only to accede to his wife's demands that they go on to Egypt. At last, on May 13, after panic had set in among depositors, Mr. Hughes arrived back in Annapolis. Old Court and Merritt Commercial went into conservatorship that evening, and the next day the governor declared an emergency and limited withdrawals from all state S&Ls. The General Assembly was called into special session. The initial panic was contained but the crisis rolled on.

Harry Hughes has taken the brunt of the criticism for this debacle, though much of it was beyond his immediate control. His handling of the first few weeks of the crisis won praise from federal officials and Special Counsel Wilbur Preston. But his tortoise-like approach since then has proved far less successful.

Time and again, the governor was pressed by top legislative leaders to accelerate the cleanup process. Yet he continued to drag his feet on submitting plans and data to the General Assembly and failed to show aggressiveness in seeking out buyers for the crippled S&Ls.

Even worse, Mr. Hughes decided to ignore the public clamor for assurances that he was indeed managing the situation well. He refused to hold press conferences for three months and adopted a vow of silence. This only fed the public's growing apprehensions and dramatically undermined their confidence in Mr. Hughes' ability to govern

The result has been a remarkable plunge in the polls. Where Mr. Hughes was once a convincing front-runner in the race for U.S. Senate, he is now a distant third. A Mason-Dixon poll last September made Mr. Hughes an easy winner in the Democratic Senate primary with 47 percent. The firm's latest poll gives him only 17 percent.

Mr. Sachs has a somewhat different problem. He would love to tell the inside story. It would help his campaign for governor to detail sleazy activities his office has uncovered. But politics and criminal prosecutions don't mix and Mr. Sachs' prosecutorial duties come first. Even when indictments are presented, Mr. Sachs will have to keep quiet until the trials are over, probably long after the September 9 primary.

Indeed, this story could go on for years. Circuit Court Judge Joseph H.H. Kaplan says he hopes to conclude all the S&L litigation by the time his term expires seven years from now, in 1993. Even then, he adds, there may still be matters unresolved. The S&L monster could celebrate many more birthdays before it finally disappears.

Chapter 3

Lord Mayor
Looks *to*
Annapolis

Lord Baltimore

September 19, 1983

All that now stands between William Donald Schaefer and his coronation as Lord of All Baltimore is the Republican Party's sacrificial lamb, Sam Culotta. Once the November election charade is over, the mayor can do what he likes doing best — ruling his realm.

He will do so with one of the most sweeping mandates ever given a Maryland politician.

Mr. Schaefer emerged the Democratic primary winner in every district in the city and he did so against an articulate but flawed black challenger who attempted to ride to City Hall on a wave of black political consciousness.

It is interesting to compare the vote totals of William H. Murphy Jr., Mr. Schaefer's main opponent this year, to those run up by Kurt Schmoke last year when Mr. Schmoke, also black, won the race for state's attorney by unifying the black community and pulling in substantial numbers of white voters. Mr. Murphy did not win a majority even in the predominantly black precincts, and he got practically no white votes.

Or compare the Murphy results to those of George L. Russell Jr., the first legitimate black mayoral candidate, back in 1971. Despite the fact that 60,000 fewer votes were cast and far fewer blacks were registered, Mr. Russell's vote total was only 1,500 short of Mr. Murphy's 1983 total. Mr. Russell managed to win 36 percent of the vote against Mr. Schaefer that year; Mr. Murphy got 26 percent this year. Mr. Russell lost by only 36,600 votes; Mr. Murphy's losing margin was 103,000.

Mr. Murphy thrust himself on the city's blacks as their messiah. What they saw of him, though, they apparently did not like very much, rejecting him while affirming their faith in Clarence (Du) Burns, a man of basic decency and integrity who, unlike Mr. Murphy, labored for years in the city's neighborhoods before emerging as Baltimore's first black City Council president.

Mr. Burns has paid his dues. And his taxes.

Should Mr. Schmoke decide to run for mayor in four years, the best advice for Mr. Murphy is to get out of the way. If anything, the state's attorney's popularity has increased since his surprise election last year.

But what lies ahead for Mayor Schaefer? Will he seek to remain in office until the 1990s? Will he be mayor for life?

Speculation already centers on a possible Schaefer-for-Governor campaign in 1986. Statewide popularity polls have put Mr. Schaefer so far ahead of any other politician that he would be foolish not to give such a race serious thought. In fact, there is evidence the mayor already has been tempted to form a statewide organization.

During this past summer's campaign, the groundwork was laid for a Marylanders for Schaefer Committee. This was to combat Mr. Murphy's importation of national black political leaders to endorse his candidacy. The willingness of politicians throughout Maryland to support the mayor was "incredible," according to one of those involved. It would have been the first step toward a run for the State House.

But then the Schaefer camp got back the results of a poll showing Mr. Murphy's import-a -politician strategy was hurting him badly among voters, black and white. Only then, with great reluctance, did the mayor agree to disband the Marylanders for Schaefer effort. Why risk angering voters already upset with Mr. Murphy's use of outsiders?

The lure of the State House probably will increase for Mr. Schaefer. Annapolis is becoming more and more a key to the city's financial fortunes. Though the three major contenders for governor — Attorney General Stephen H. Sachs, House Speaker Benjamin L. Cardin and Baltimore County Executive Donald P. Hutchinson — are big Baltimore boosters, they do not share Mr. Schaefer's fanatic determination to tilt state policy sharply toward the city.

Given the mayor's growing anger and frustration with the Hughes administration's lackadaisical attitude toward the city, he may want very much to be the next resident of the governor's mansion three years hence.

Billy Murphy and George Russell continue to practice law in Baltimore. Sam Culotta is still active in the Republican Party. Du Burns, after serving as interim mayor in 1987, is in retirement.

Two defenders of "One Maryland"

November 7, 1985

Stephen Sachs' gubernatorial campaign slogan is "One Maryland." It could just as easily be William Donald Schaefer's. But Mr. Schaefer's "One Maryland" bears little resemblance to the one envisaged by Mr. Sachs.

What Attorney General Sachs is trying to stress to voters a year before the general election is the importance of seeing Maryland as a single, integrated entity, not as 24 independent subdivisions. Only then can the next governor meet the special problems of certain areas without creating a political uproar. That's the Sachs message – on the surface. There's a subliminal message, too.

"One Maryland" is a subtle way of telling people in the suburbs and beyond that under a Sachs administration in Annapolis, benefits will be dispensed more evenly to all parts of the state, not just to "special pleaders" from Baltimore.

Mr. Sachs hotly denies any intent to run an anti-Baltimore campaign, but his message conveys a different impression. Part of his campaign strategy is to capitalize on traditional rural/urban animosity.

The mayor, Mr. Sachs intimates, doesn't understand the problems of Montgomery County and Prince George's County and Cumberland and Easton and Leonardtown. The impression he's trying to create is that the mayor's interests in becoming governor begin and end with increased aid for Baltimore City.

The city (Schaefer) against the rest of the state (Sachs).

It is a difficult trick for the attorney general to pull off, since he himself is a born and bred Baltimorean whose family and personal ties to the city are strong.

But Mr. Sachs has spent the last seven years as attorney general, establishing a record as an elected *state* official. Among the senior state officials, only the ubiquitous Louis Goldstein has seen more of Maryland during that time. Mr. Sachs wants to be known as a *Maryland* candidate.

This would be a fine strategy were he running against someone who is perceived as a regional candidate. Mr. Schaefer is attempting to avoid that pitfall by campaigning as Maryland's favorite mayor who wants the chance to duplicate his Baltimore miracles in Annapolis. Mr. Schaefer tells audiences that Maryland "has to be a state where everyone works together to make it greater than it is." Each county and each city are interrelated, he tells them. The special needs of all subdivisions can be met by a unified Maryland.

It is a vision of "One Maryland" in which "special pleaders" are not disparaged but heeded, in which the weak are helped out by the strong, in which vigorous programs are launched to spur economic development throughout the state, but especially where it is most needed.

The mayor uses his accomplishments in Baltimore as an example of what he can do for the state: People working together have pulled the city back from the edge of the abyss. The Baltimore renaissance has drawn national attention. "It can work on the state level," he tells audiences.

Baltimore is the key issue.

To Mr. Schaefer, Baltimore's deeds should become an example for the rest of the state. Marylanders need to pay more attention, not less, to the successes and problems of the city. A growing, prospering Baltimore is central to the economic growth of the rest of the state.

To Mr. Sachs, "Baltimore cannot go it alone. Baltimore cannot be an island." The city must be willing to share more of the state's local funds with other subdivisions. That is the only way to change the hostile attitude many state politicians have toward assisting the city.

In the Schaefer vision, an understanding state comes to Baltimore's rescue, knowing that this approach will pay rewarding economic dividends.

The Sachs vision sees an understanding Baltimore dropping it parochial pleas and taking the position that what's good for Maryland is good for the city.

What does "One Maryland" mean?

It depends on which candidate for governor you're listening to.

Steve Sachs practices law in Washington.

Camelot Quest in Maryland

June 5, 1986

Ah, for the days of Camelot! When Jack and Jackie were photographed in the Rose Garden with John-John and Caroline. When young Steve Sachs was a crusading prosecutor defending truth, justice and the American way. When liberal idealism was the foundation of the New Frontier and the Peace Corps. That was a quarter-century ago. And yet Steve Sachs remains faithful to those ideals, convinced that Marylanders still feel as deeply about them as he does. His campaign for governor is a referendum on the liberalism of state voters.

He is not alone. Two politicians straight out of the New Deal-New Frontier tradition, Representatives Barbara Mikulski and Michael Barnes, are battling with two moderates in the Democratic Senate primary.

A dedicated liberal, Councilwoman Esther Gelman, is a leading congressional candidate in Montgomery County, along with a liberal name from the 1960s, former Representative Carlton Sickles.

A basketball star with no prior elective experience, Tom McMillen, sees voters in Anne Arundel County and northern Prince Georges County shifting away from their conservative tendencies to support his liberal notions in his bid for Congress.

And in Baltimore County and southern Harford County, a 34-year-old daughter of the late Robert F. Kennedy is running for Congress on the Kennedy/Camelot coattails.

Kathleen Kennedy Townsend sounded more like her father and uncle than a new, fresh voice at her campaign kickoff, declaring the challenge to be "that each of us can do better" and her belief in a "renewed spirit of volunteerism... The essence... is not giving part of our surplus we don't need; it is giving part of ourselves."

Yes, liberals — the old-fashioned variety — are testing the political tolerance of Marylanders. Forget about the Reagan sweep in the state last time, they are saying. Forget the fact that four of the state's eight congressmen are conservatives. This is still liberal territory. There is no better example than Mr. Sachs' race for governor. In choosing retiring Representative Parren Mitchell as his running mate, Mr. Sachs sent his campaign swinging to the far left of the political spectrum.

It was a calculated gamble designed to reinvigorate a campaign stuck in neutral, to mobilize a huge outpouring of black support, and to focus the gubernatorial debate on Mr. Sachs' chosen turf — civil rights, expanded government services, and the failure of his opponent, Mayor William Donald Schaefer, to bring the prosperity of Harborplace to inner-city slums.

In the short run, the Sachs announcement has succeeded in attracting enormous media attention and excitement. It has renewed the hopes of his campaign workers.

But will it last?

Are state voters interested in the issues that the Sachs-Mitchell ticket wants to discuss?

Are voters who favored Ronald Reagan, Helen Bentley, Beverly Byron, Marjorie Holt and Roy Dyson going to accept the angry, liberal rhetoric of Mr. Sachs' running mate?

Are black voters ready to abandon Mr. Schaefer's successful, pragmatic approach to government just because Mr. Sachs has picked a popular black to fill a figurehead post in his administration?

Are Jewish voters as liberal as they were 25 years ago, and will they overlook Mr. Mitchell's inflammatory remarks of the 1960s and early 1970s?

Mr. Sachs is paddling his canoe in a different direction from either the Hughes administration or the Reagan administration.

For instance, the "Sachs tax" for better education could be just the start of more tax-hike requests to pay for a formidable war on poverty in Maryland. Yet it would occur at the same time as federal efforts to drastically lower federal taxes and would run counter to Governor Hughes' long-running efforts to avoid raising state taxes.

The attorney general believes in activism. Instead of deregulating and reducing the intrusive scope of government as recent political leaders have done, Mr. Sachs talks about re-regulation and greater protection of consumers through government intervention. He is approaching this campaign as though little has changed since the early 1960s.

Mr. Sachs is either a visionary or he is trapped in a time warp. Not since Theodore Roosevelt McKeldin resided in the governor's mansion 30 years ago has this state elected a passionately liberal chief executive. Since then, every governor has been a moderate or a pragmatic conservative. Will Mr. Sachs make a breakthrough? The odds remain heavily against him. Camelot still seems a distant memory.

Kathleen Kennedy Townsend was elected lieutenant governor in 1994. Tom McMillen served in Congress from 1986 through 1990.

Old Mayor, New Governor

January 25, 1987

The best contribution William Donald Schaefer could have made to Baltimore City was to leave its familiar environs. He continues to be Baltimore's biggest booster, but now he has a more lofty — and influential — position in another city. Mr. Schaefer had just about run through his bag of tricks as Baltimore's long-time mayor. The city's financial base continues to slip relative to affluent surrounding counties. It continues to be home to most of the state's poor, its homeless, its elderly and its disabled. Despite success with downtown rejuvenation, luring taxpaying firms into the city is difficult. The appeal of the suburbs is hard to overcome.

In his 15 years as mayor, Mr. Schaefer acted as Baltimore's chief cheerleader and financial tightwad. He lifted spirits and erased the city's psychological depression. He clamped down on spending in order to keep the property-tax rate, by far the highest in Maryland, from reaching onerous levels. He devised imaginative ways to finance costly projects. He pleaded and begged and cajoled governors and presidents to send more assistance to Baltimore.

The Schaefer performance worked — up to a point. This aging urban center still remains a city with monumental troubles. Its financially strapped schools rate no better than a C-minus. Its infrastructure (roads, bridges, sewers) is crumbling from age and there are insufficient funds to make costly repairs. The upper middle class, both black and white, continues to move to the suburbs.

And on top of these woes, federal aid to the cities has declined sharply under the Reagan budget knife and the Gramm-Rudman-Hollings budget-reduction law.

In such a situation, what could a mayor do to help his city? He could

resign to become governor.

Annapolis may not be Fort Knox, but the state treasury is bulging compared with the city's.

In fact, state government has surpassed Washington as the biggest supplier of funds for the city. The total amount of money flowing from Annapolis to Baltimore even surpasses the amount of revenue raised locally from the property tax.

So Mr. Schaefer's desire to jump from mayor to governor was a logical progression for the city-minded leader. He won't be able to stage a raid on the state treasury, but he is in a position to steer more funds in Baltimore's direction.

He already has started to do so. His first budget, released Friday, proposes a sizable increase in education aid, based on a formula that favors the city. He also wants much of the surplus from income-tax changes to go into social-service programs that do much of their work in the city.

Mr. Schaefer intends to push hard for one or two new stadiums for Baltimore, a move he and others believe would give tremendous impetus to the city's downtown development as a business, tourist and entertainment center.

The stadium bill probably faced no better than 50-50 prospects during the Hughes era; under the Schaefer regime, the odds of the General Assembly approving such legislation are probably 2-1.

Why? Because Mr. Schaefer will use the power and prestige of his position to promote the idea. He will turn the office into a "bully pulpit." Mr. Hughes was never enthusiastic or deeply committed to a new sports complex. Mr. Schaefer is.

This governor will have his official residence in Annapolis (required by the Constitution) but his unofficial home in West Baltimore. The governor of Maryland will be seen cavorting in the city frequently, holding press conferences and other events here. The State Office Building complex will be elevated in status, with the governor often working out of his suite of offices there.

New state agencies probably will move into the city. Under the Hughes administration, the Department of Economic and Community Development chose Annapolis over Baltimore for its headquarters, in part because the cabinet secretary liked the capital's ambience and convenience. This would never have happened had Mr. Schaefer been governor at the time.

The proposed cabinet-level housing department is almost certain to be located in the city. Other agencies with administrative offices in the Baltimore suburbs probably will be told to do the same once their leases expire.

Also, look for an acceleration of construction on the Arundel Freeway linking Annapolis and Baltimore. As Mr. Schaefer and his many resident-Baltimore aides are discovering, the commute via clogged Ritchie Highway can take hours, especially in weather such as last week's snowstorm. That means wasting large chunks of the working day stuck in traffic. The short-tempered, "do it now" governor won't be happy with this situation.

The result could be fast work to complete the freeway, which could tie the two cities closer together, spur economic development and provide countless synergetic benefits. A light-rail transit line to Annapolis is another candidate for priority status.

When he entered the historic State House for his inauguration last week, Mr. Schaefer appeared apprehensive and awed. As mayor, he was one of hundreds of similarly elected officials. As governor, he is one of only 50. The tradition and majesty of the office is, indeed, impressive. But Mr. Schaefer had to make the move, despite his apprehension. He has invested too much of his life in Baltimore's well-being to have done anything else.

'OUT OF THE WAY, PEASANT... THE GOVERNOR FROM ANNAPOLIS IS HERE!'

Chapter 4

Schaefer
Triumphant

The Schaefer – Schmoke Feud

December 13, 1985

If you want to know why William Donald Schaefer is steamed at Baltimore's new mayor, Kurt L. Schmoke, look no further than Mayor Schmoke's first day in office.

The mayor gained Board of Estimates approval for 27 new staff jobs and big pay boosts for his top aides, at an annual cost of $1 million. Nary a peep of protest was heard. When Governor-elect Schaefer tried to do the same thing last January, requesting 31 new positions costing $1 million, he was met with adamant opposition from outgoing Governor Harry Hughes, harsh legislative and press condemnation and accusations of being power-hungry and arrogant.

Or take another recent example: Mr. Schmoke unceremoniously dumped several cabinet-level officials and fired dozens of staffers in the mayor's office. Again, no one seemed to mind the large-scale firings or the abrupt dismissal notices for top city appointees.

Yet when Mr. Schaefer became governor and *retained* a surprisingly large number of Hughes officials, the new governor received no applause. Instead, he was lambasted for bringing in his own personal staff from Baltimore and hiring a number of cabinet secretaries who had worked for him in the city.

It's Kurt Schmoke, the golden boy of Maryland politics, versus William Donald Schaefer, who never seems to get the respect he feels he deserves. This may not be the cause of the Schmoke-Schaefer rift, but it is a major reason the governor made sure he was in Emmitsburg watching a basketball game last week when Mr. Schmoke was sworn in.

The governor rightly points out that Mr. Schmoke never seems to get ripped by the press or by politicians; he has a good-guy image and usually avoids creating a stir. He has a shyness and Teflon quality Ronald Reagan would envy.

Compare that with Mr. Schaefer. He is impetuous, not shy. His "do it now" style of governing is a lightning rod for controversy. Yet Mr. Schaefer has shown himself extraordinarily thin-skinned to even the slightest whiff of criticism.

The styles of the two men don't mesh. Mr. Schaefer has an eight-year accumulation of grievances against Mr. Schmoke, most of them petty. Mr. Schmoke, as Baltimore's state's attorney, didn't attend all Schaefer cabinet meetings; when he did come he was inattentive, late or nodded off; he went to the press to complain about a budget cut rather than working it out quietly; he regularly slighted the mayor.

All of these sins might have been forgiven had not Mr. Schmoke made a dumb political move: He endorsed Mr. Schaefer's gubernatorial foe, Stephen H. Sachs. In the closing weeks of the campaign he taped a radio commercial that urged voters to support Mr. Sachs.

Some of Mr. Schmoke's advisers tried to dissuade him from making the commercial. Why go out of your way to antagonize the next governor? Mr. Schmoke — who remains surprisingly naive for a successful politician — wouldn't listen. The damage from the endorsement commercial cannot be understated.

Reconciliation has proved fruitless. Mr. Schmoke makes occasional stabs through intermediaries, but Mr. Schaefer remains deeply embittered. What is needed is a private meeting in which the two men thrash out their misgivings and find a way to cooperate. Mr. Schaefer took this route with the Reverend Wendell Phillips and Delegate Larry Young with outstanding results.

There is a danger in this rift that is quite real: If the governor turns his back on the mayor's requests for help, the city of Baltimore will suffer. Mr. Schaefer doesn't have nearly enough money to meet the most pressing state needs; making room for additional city aid would be a difficult political task even under a supportive governor.

Mr. Schaefer feels that Mr. Schmoke has had it easy. He was a star football player and class president at City College high school, a student-athlete at Yale, a Rhodes scholar, an Ivy League law student, a White House aide, a lawyer in a prestigious firm, a landslide winner (twice) for state's attorney. Success has come naturally to him.

By contrast, Mr. Schaefer's road has been anything but smooth: high school diploma from City College; night school at the University of Baltimore law school; a stint in the Army; humdrum real-estate work with two law partners; two defeats for House of Delegates; four terms in the City Council, including one term as Council president, and four terms as mayor. He's had to fight his way up without the glamour and "star" quality attached to Mr. Schmoke.

Mr. Schaefer is 66; Mr. Schmoke is 38. They represent different political generations. Mr. Schaefer sees himself as the old-fashioned, nose-to-the-grindstone, blue-collar politician. It's his whole life. Mr. Schmoke, in Mr. Schaefer's eyes, is the consummate yuppie (complete with a professional wife and two children) who doesn't know what it means to work day and night for decades as a public servant.

Now Mr. Schaefer is determined to see that Mr. Schmoke learns how tough it is to be mayor, especially a mayor without a friend in the governor's mansion. Mr. Schaefer suffered for eight years during Mr. Hughes' reign as governor; now the new governor is hinting he'll be the same kind of anti-city ogre he so detested in Mr. Hughes.

Is that fair? No, but Mr. Schaefer doesn't seem to care. His emotions and his feelings — for now — are ruling his actions. Don't count on Kurt Schmoke to be invited to the governor's Christmas party. Not this year, anyway.

Schaefer Rages to Get What He Wants

March 6, 1988

Is Governor William Donald Schaefer simply a "66-year-old-baby," as one longtime political observer put it, or a crafty politician using outbursts of anger to get his way?

That's the question legislators and friends of the governor now are asking themselves. Mr. Schaefer in the past has been prone to periods of rage, but he has quickly calmed down.

This time, the governor's fury continued far longer than normal — both privately and publicly. He erupted over budget subcommittee cuts, the appointment of a bond counsel to the stadium authority and even over unfavorable newspaper articles. A staff retreat last weekend did nothing to help matters: His aides reinforced his prejudices against the legislature and the notion that it's "them against us."

By week's end, though, the eruption of Mount Schaefer had subsided and the governor was talking soothingly about patching things up with legislators. "I've got an ego that's as big as any of 'em," he conceded on a radio call-in show, "and I guess these clashes of ego are right tough. But the most important thing is to set those egos aside and get things like light rail moving."

That Mr. Schaefer would act this way comes as no surprise to those who have closely followed his career. But his outbursts in Baltimore were never fully reported. Only occasionally did Mr. Schaefer slip up in public, like the time he called one South Baltimore councilman a "dumb son of a bitch."

Now Mr. Schaefer is in the fish bowl. Nearly every comment he makes is reported. He is under constant scrutiny, especially during the 90-day session of the General Assembly. It is an extraordinarily tough job. And often a thankless one.

Mr. Schaefer does not take criticism well. He is sensitive to perceived slights. Lawmakers didn't understand that. The swings they took at the gov-

WILLIAM DONALD SCHAEFER
TIMPANIST

ernor last year — especially vicious swipes from Senate President Thomas V. Mike Miller — deeply offended Mr. Schaefer. It shaped his perception of the legislature as "the enemy."

Yet despite the governor's rantings, his legislative package is progressing nicely. In fact, the situation is strikingly similar to the governor's first confrontation with the legislature a year ago.

As the midway point in the 1987 General Assembly session, Mr. Schaefer was frustrated and worried. His "do it now" approach was running into a legislative roadblock. His plan to spend most of the federal income-tax windfall coming Maryland's way on social service programs for the poor and helpless had been rebuffed. It looked as though everything on the governor's agenda would be rejected.

But after angrily bemoaning his plight, the governor calmed down and began cooperating with legislators. He talked with them individually. He was warm and friendly. He offered support for pet bills in exchange for support on administration proposals. He won them over with his charm, sincerity and honesty. By adjournment night Mr. Schaefer had achieved just about everything he wanted. It was a sensational session for a rookie governor.

This time around, the same pattern is emerging. True, the governor's pet plan for a residential math-science high school was killed, but it never had much support in the legislature, anyway. Some of the governor's proposed slush funds bit the dust, too. Virtually every other administration initiative, though, is moving through the legislative maze.

There's even reason to hope a higher-education restructuring bill might have a shot at passage.

Some proposals have been toned down — such as the light-rail line for metropolitan Baltimore and an economic development "sunny day" fund. They should pass, though.

Three years from now, no one will remember these initial funding battles. The programs will be in full swing and are likely to be regarded as great Schaefer accomplishments. If Governor Schaefer's long-term objective is to change the face of Maryland for the better, he is well on his way toward achieving that goal.

As mayor of Baltimore, Mr. Schaefer dealt with a meek and powerless legislative body. The City Council never made a substantial cut in his budget. It never killed any of his bills. This went on for 15 years. No wonder Mr. Schaefer has found life in Annapolis difficult. After batting .900 for so long, it's tough to adjust to a new league where a .650 batting average is considered superb.

Mr. Schaefer is being asked to change his style. That's not easy for anyone. He is learning the hard way how to do it.

In the process he has become the center of attention, the person everyone is trying to placate. That may have been Mr. Schaefer's motive all along. No one is likely to pick a fight purposely with the governor any time soon.

Going Nuts over Guns

Novemner 6, 1988

What has triggered such overwhelming interest in Maryland's handgun law? Why has the National Rifle Association poured some $5 million into Maryland in an effort to kill the law? Why have major officeholders in the state, church groups, medical groups and police groups made this *the* issue of the November 8 election?

Sociologists will have a field day answering those questions. Clearly, this gun referendum has hit a nerve. Marylanders are exercised, be they fanatically opposed to the handgun law or adamantly in favor of it. Everyone seems to feel strongly, one way or the other. Why all the fuss?

Crime has become a dominant theme in campaigns this year, especially the race for president and the handgun battle.

People are worried about the proliferation of crimes of violence, most of them drug-related, and the growing use of handguns. There are a million firearms registered in Maryland and at least that many more guns illegally owned. An alarming spate of handgun incidents in Baltimore City schools this fall has alarmed parents and baffled school officials. Shootings are on the rise in the Maryland suburbs, and even rural areas are witnessing an increase in crimes involving firearms.

It seems to many people that society is on the verge of losing control. Baltimore Mayor Kurt Schmoke's call for a debate to legalize the sale of drugs sent the sad message that even the city's top elected official is ready to admit defeat. The bad guys look like they are winning.

The drive to do something to thwart criminals gathered surprising momentum during the General Assembly session last spring. Legislators took a pragmatic approach — egged on by angry constituents demanding action. They passed a law designed to stop the sale and ownership of cheap, easily concealable Saturday Night Specials, weapons favored by street criminals and teen-age hoodlums.

It seemed a sensible thing to do. But to satisfy NRA objections, the bill was watered down substantially. The very changes that the NRA insisted upon in the spring became the NRA's basis for charges during the summer and fall that the handgun law was fatally flawed.

This hypocrisy has mattered little to the NRA. It launched Maryland's most costly campaign — by far — to kill the law on referendum. The tactics being employed will go down in political-science textbooks as a classic use of distortion, misinformation and fear to sway voters. This expensive propaganda drive has left little room for an objective discussion of the issue.

Gun lovers care very deeply about their right to own firearms. They view it as a constitutional right — though the courts and some scholars might disagree with that interpretation. Still, to these people the handgun law represents the first move toward state control of such weapons. It may seem an unreasonable fear, even a paranoid fear, but to these patriotic Americans any move that hints at gun confiscation is to be resisted to the nth degree.

The hysteria of the NRA's attack has only intensified the determination of those backing the law. With the NRA outspending gun-law backers 10-1, supporters have turned to high-visibility media events, carefully timing their press conferences to get maximum exposure. The strategy has been effective in reducing the NRA's clear advantage in paid advertising, which has seemed to inundate the air waves in the final month of the campaign.

Thus both sides have manipulated the media in their own ways. And both have been successful, in their own ways.

Why all this interest in the handgun vote? Because violence is a pivotal social issue in modern America. Marylanders are attempting, through classic democratic means, to reconcile the provisions of an 18th-century Constitution with a 20th-century threat to public safety. It isn't an easy task.

Regardless of the outcome, Tuesday's vote on the handgun referendum won't end the debate. The losing side will see to that.

Marylanders overwhelmingly approved the handgun-control law in November 1988 by a margin of 264,000 votes.

Never Say Never Involved

July 16, 1989

He's back! Just when you thought it was safe to go back in the water, the great white shark has reappeared. And he's ready for more action!

This isn't a billing for "Jaws 4." It's a reference to Maryland's newest addition to the state bar, Marvin "Buddy" Mandel.

Some of you might remember Mr. Mandel. He used to be governor. A pretty good one, too. Only trouble was, he cut a few corners and made sure his friends were well taken care of when the state doled out favors. He was nabbed by the feds for political corruption and (after a few false starts) convicted by a jury of his peers.

He spent 19 months in the slammer, albeit at one of those "country club" prisons in sunny Florida. Since getting out, he's been trying to win vindication. He also apparently managed to earn a very comfortable living as a "consultant" to a Severna Park contracting company.

Finally, after a 12-year battle, the courts last month threw out Mr. Mandel's conviction on a technicality. He had been found guilty of acts no longer viewed as illegal under the new court interpretation of the federal mail-fraud statute. What Mr. Mandel did (essentially taking favors from friends and then helping them out) remains unchanged; but now such behavior is condoned by the federal courts.

Marylanders will have to decide for themselves whether Mr. Mandel's conduct was ethically and morally proper. The state bar and the Court of Appeals seem to think everything is on the up and up. They wasted no time a week ago giving Mr. Mandel a ringing endorsement and their seal of approval. Now he can once again hang out his "attorney" shingle.

Marvin Mandel was the best and last great practitioner of the old b'hoy style of State House politics. (The lone remnant of that era, Paul Weisengoff, has never lived up to expectations and remains a secondary figure on the

Annapolis scene.) He was a master at manipulating and cajoling legislators. He became the "let's make a deal" maestro of the State House, always able to figure out some Machiavellian way to beat the odds and get what he wanted. And he was great newspaper copy. Mr. Mandel had a colorless personality but a deviousness that fascinated reporters. He fought giant legislative battles and won nearly all of them. His loud and messy divorce caused a national sensation. He was always dabbling in something that teetered on the edge of impropriety.

Mr. Mandel also had a knack for obscuring his intentions. He'd take a few puffs on his meerschaum pipe, nod his head and two legislators in the room would come away with wildly differing interpretations of what the governor had said.

His press conferences were studies in obscurantism. Reporters called his comments "Buddyisms." He has a novel way with words.

Take his famous "not involved" statement. Reporters were badgering him in 1975 about his involvement in a sleazy race track deal that netted millions for his friends. He was asked if these friends had ever mentioned to him their hidden financial role, which prosecutors were investigating.

"No, sir."

Why hadn't he asked them about it when the questions arose?

His answer was a classic example of Buddyism:

"I'm not getting involved; I am not involved; I have never been involved and I don't intend to get involved in any phase of any of that. I have no intention of asking any questions of anybody because I don't want to be accused of doing anything that would involve me with anyone who has at any time had their name in the paper involved with that situation. So I am not asking any questions of anyone."

One legislative reporter was so moved by the symmetry of this soliloquy that he turned it into a poem ("Involved") and placed a copy on the press room wall, where it remained for nearly a decade — a bizarre memorial to a State House legend.

But now, he's back! It's like old times: His name and picture are sprawled all over the newspapers. Reporters are calling him. And he's got a new slant on his "involved" statement.

A reporter asked if he would keep his hand in state politics. His response deserves the same kind of poetic treatment he received 14 years ago:

INVOLVED II
By M. Buddy Mandel

There's no question
I will be
Involved.
I've always been

Involved.
I've never really
Gotten away from being
Involved.

With a law practice to call his own, with his good pal William Donald Schaefer in the governor's chair and with a burning desire to reclaim a spot in the political arena, Marvin Mandel will be popping up more and more frequently in the State House. The great white shark is on the prowl once again.

Marvin Mandel practices law and lobbies in Annapolis.

Leading to Regional Horizons

October 8, 1989

There may yet be a rapprochement between Montgomery County and Baltimore City. Not immediately, but sometime in the 1990s. Let's hope it occurs, because Baltimore badly needs a strong ally like Montgomery.

Montgomery County is the new, unrivaled economic engine of Maryland. In recent years, it has generated 34 percent of the state's population growth and 21 percent of the state's new jobs.

The problem Montgomery faces is how to cope with its success. It is having trouble doing so — clamping down on new development, putting up tens of millions in local money to accelerate road and school construction the state won't pay for, mulling over how to control its future without shutting out the economic growth that has made Montgomery the most affluent county in the country. But what of Montgomery's obligations to Baltimore and the rest of Maryland? Does charity begin — and end — at home?

I was asked to debate that question before a group of young executives and community representatives at the inaugural session of Leadership Montgomery, modeled after the Greater Baltimore Committee's successful Leadership program for up-and-coming area leaders. Most interesting was the response of those in the audience afterward. No one wanted to build a wall around Montgomery and let the rest of the state take care of itself. No one was anxious to see Baltimore disintegrate. No one advocated "benign neglect."

Instead, many of these young Montgomery leaders demanded to know why the city had failed to put a quality school system at the top of it priority list.

How could the Schaefer administration have let the schools decline into such disarray? Why hasn't the Schmoke administration done more to turn things around? Why was Baltimore putting its money elsewhere?

It didn't make sense to them, and it made them angry. In Montgomery, quality schooling is the *sine qua non* of all residents. They recognize that a solid education translates into a good job and a good life. If a community will not insist upon good schools for its own children, why should rich subdivisions come to its rescue? That is a valid point. The key question is whether the Schmoke administration understands this point and whether the mayor is capable of giving education the kind of special financial priority it warrants. It is probably the only way of convincing legislators in Annapolis to approve more state aid. A greater city commitment — and financial sacrifice — is imperative.

Happily, these young Montgomery leaders were more interested in making the future work than rehashing the past. They wanted to discuss solutions, not historic conflicts. Yes, Montgomery's own interests come first. But this rich county still retains a deep social conscience. Finding a way to tap that reservoir of good will is the city's challenge.

Some of the participants wanted to know how to reach out and discuss the city's dilemma directly with people in Baltimore. They were eager to "network" with their counterparts. Why let politicians engage in futile wrangling when community and corporate leaders can work out ways to help the city?

It could be quite simple. Earlier in the day, the group had toured the National Geographic Society's spectacular Gaithersburg building, where the conference was held, and learned that the society farms out its data-processing work — to North Carolina. That's 400 to 500 jobs which could just as easily have been directed to impoverished Baltimore.

If a couple of dozen big companies in Montgomery decided to pursue such a helping-hand strategy, it might mean 10,000 new city jobs — a huge shot in the arm for Baltimore at no cost to Montgomery taxpayers.

With the Baltimore and Washington regions rapidly blending together, a Baltimore-Montgomery dialogue is inevitable. Unless something is done to stem the city's downward spiral, it will turn into a millstone around the neck of the Baltwash (or Washbalt, if you prefer) economy.

There are plenty of painless and innovative ways for the rich county to help the poor city, especially if the private sector is involved. Politicians seem to relish the kind of angry, confrontational rhetoric that has pitted the two subdivisions against one another in the State House. It has been a fruitless, destructive endeavor. It hasn't rescued Baltimore from what appears to be a bleak future. A little "networking" from folks like those in Leadership Montgomery might, though.

Mikey, Mikey!

December 10, 1989

Mikey, Mikey, Mikey. What have you done to yourself? What should have been a high point in Senate President Thomas V. Mike Miller's career — a huge $250-a-ticket fundraiser — quickly turned to mush, thanks to his unseemly and profane comments about living conditions in Baltimore City. The morning after his linguistic misadventures, Mr. Miller tried to put Humpty-Dumpty back together again, only to conclude, "Today is the worst day of my life."

Now the Senate leader is filled with remorse. He'd do anything to erase that taped television interview, the one with his unflattering descriptions of Charm City. By the time guests were filtering into the Miller fundraiser that evening, all the local television stations had replayed The Tape. Camera crews descended on Mr. Miller and Governor William Donald Schaefer for reaction, bringing the receiving line to a standstill. The general consensus that evening: Mike had put his foot in his mouth once again.

At age 47, Mike Miller is youthful looking and youthful in his behavior. He's still a devotee of rock musician Frank Zappa. He's a fanatical follower of his alma mater's (College Park) athletic teams. He's a friendly, back-slapping, small-town lawyer from still-rural Clinton in Prince George's County.

The problem is that he doesn't know when to keep his mouth shut. And he still doesn't understand that a politician has to take great care before telling journalists what he *really* thinks.

It was Mr. Miller who used the first day of his first General Assembly session as Senate president to calmly tell reporters that the new governor was acting like a dictatorial brat. So much for bridge-building between a new chief executive and a new legislative leader.

And it was Mr. Miller who embarrassed colleagues that session at the annual Legislative Follies by delivering a profane and inappropriate monologue concerning the governor and his companion, Hilda Mae Snoops — both of whom were in the audience: It was a dumb thing to do (Mr. Miller thought it would be received humorously). Mr. Schaefer, as is his habit, has not forgotten.

Mike Miller continues to act as though he were back at the University of Maryland exchanging obscene wise-cracks with the boys on Fraternity Row. His sophomoric hi-jinks might be gleefully celebrated there, but not in the State House. He has become a walking time bomb: you never know when he's going to detonate while chatting with reporters.

The irony of this latest controversy is that Mr. Miller had no intentions of dumping on Baltimore when he made his comments. He was trying to describe the depths of the city's problems to show why the city needs more help from Annapolis. It didn't come off that way. Now he's desperate to make amends.

His predicament illustrates the central role Baltimore continues to play in Maryland politics, regardless of the population change that is shifting more power to the suburbs. Baltimore remains a key to winning statewide office. Mike Miller can't do it without Baltimore, and neither can any other politician.

If you are identified as having an anti-Baltimore bias, you're going to lose the city and most of the surrounding counties — and with them the election. This is likely to remain true well into the next decade, and maybe even into the next century.

Only the Baltimore television stations give constant attention to what's happening in Annapolis and around the state. Only the Baltimore newspapers give regular, timely and in-depth coverage to the General Assembly, the governor and the state. Baltimore is the media center for Maryland politicians; Washington outlets barely compete in this arena.

No wonder, then, that Mike Miller was contrite. He'd like to be governor or lieutenant governor or attorney general some day. But now there is The Tape. Who's going to back him, or put him on a statewide ticket, when opponents are sure to re-broadcast The Tape and attack Mr. Miller for his low blow?

Who is going to take the chance of picking a running mate with a proclivity for ribald or immature comments that could outrage voters? So Mr. Miller is left in the position of holding $350,000 from his fundraiser and nowhere to spend it. He may have to revamp his long-range political plans.

His best approach would be to adopt Baltimore as a special project. As Senate president, and as legislative leader of the county with the state's second-largest black population, Mr. Miller could be the catalyst for a Prince George's-Baltimore City alliance. He could be the prime mover of an enlightened help-the-city drive in the General Assembly.

The Tape might eventually be forgotten, eclipsed by Mr. Miller's numerous good deeds for the city. Besides, voters have a short political memory and Mr. Miller has a long political life ahead of him. He'll be only 51 when Governor Schaefer finishes his second term, only 59 when Mickey Steinberg finishes *his* second term, and a mere 67 when Kurt Schmoke ends *his* second gubernatorial term in 2010.

Mike Miller continues to serve as president of the Maryland State Senate.

Sinking Deeper in the Bog

December 24, 1989

This has been a bummer of a year for Maryland higher education.
Nineteen eighty-nine started out with an intense behind-the-scenes struggle between the University of Maryland's chancellor and board chairman. It is ending with an equally tenacious behind-the-scenes struggle between UM's new interim-chancellor and the chairman of the Maryland Higher Education Commission.

Spaced between these two events have been traumatic upheavals and internal warfare. Out of all this comes little for which to rejoice. If anything, higher education in Maryland ends the year in a deeper quagmire than ever.

Here's what was supposed to happen: Governor William Donald Schaefer, dissatisfied with the paucity of sterling public colleges in Maryland, put his considerable muscle behind a reorganization of the state's higher education system in 1988.

The boards were created to bring cohesion and focus to public academics. The boards were supposed to knock heads together and make tough decisions that might infuriate educators but which would give Maryland a more rational higher education setup.

Peter O'Malley, a former UM board chairman and a savvy political strategist, was to serve as its headmaster. He handpicked UM's new regents. He was to provide the impetus for change as its chairman.

That involved a series of difficult objectives: loosening Chancellor John Toll's stranglehold on the board of regents; developing a consensus for reform among members of the new board, and zeroing in on ways to upgrade higher education, especially in the Baltimore and Washington suburbs.

The Toll-O'Malley imbroglio dragged on until summer's end, when the chancellor finally left. It sidetracked Mr. O'Malley from concentrating on his larger goals. By the time the regents started discussing the fate of individual campuses, they were in a sprint to complete work by October 1. This rush led to Mr. O'Malley's fatal blunder: he tried to push too quickly for a sweeping three-campus Baltimore merger, well before he had gained a firm foundation of support from key educators and politicians.

The result: the president-designate of one Baltimore-area campus angrily quit; politically manipulative academics pointed an accusing finger at Mr. O'Malley for being too politically manipulative; and Mr. O'Malley gave the academics what they wanted — his head.

His resignation from the board left the regents rudderless. Mr. O'Malley had been the regents' driving force. Since his departure, the panel has drifted listlessly, unwilling to offend any academics or resume serious consideration of what ails the UM system.

Meanwhile, the other higher education board, with the ungainly acronym of MHEC, began flexing its muscles.

The commission's chairman, Henry Butta, is a hard-driving corporate CEO who wants to be the one to dictate higher education changes and advise his friend the governor on these issues. He has clashed repeatedly with UM's interim chancellor, Dolph Norton, over who should call the shots on such matters as campus budgets, planning and determining strategy.

As Mr. Norton is discovering, Maryland-style higher education is a minefield even for the most skilled education administrators. Not only is higher education a political football for each campus' vocal constituency, but the Schaefer-inspired restructuring has made matters worse — not better — by imposing two governing boards on top of the campus structure. It is a Rube Goldberg creation seemingly designed to spawn eternal stress.

So, where does higher education stand on this Christmas Eve?

UM's board of regents appears content to let the bickering and turf-protective administrators have their way.

MHEC is still searching for its proper role.

Acting UM Chancellor Norton is attempting to bring a semblance of order to this jumble before he leaves in mid-1990.

And each campus is scrambling to be first in line for a bigger slice of the financial pie, regardless of what's best for the overall structure.

If that sounds like *deja vu*, it is. Higher education in Maryland seems to be moving in reverse. It's "back to the future" for the academic knights of this quixotic roundtable.

Peter O'Malley, once a power in Prince George's County politics, has been active in legal and business circles. John Toll is president of Washington College in Chestertown.

The '80s of Hughes and Schaefer

December 31, 1989

Two men dominated the Maryland scene during the 1980s, men who were remarkable in their successes and in their differences. They defined the decade, which in this state was marked by continuing prosperity and a major financial scandal.

Harry Hughes and William Donald Schaefer are polar opposites. Mr. Hughes is cool and reserved; Mr. Schaefer is hot-tempered and out-spoken. Mr. Hughes had served for two decades in state government before becoming governor; Mr. Schaefer had no state expertise. Mr. Hughes believed in cautious, incremental progress and conservative fiscal policies; Mr. Schaefer likes to go for broke and scorns piecemeal advances or hold-tight spending.

Yet Maryland prospered in the 1980s under both men. Mr. Hughes deferred many gubernatorial decisions to legislative leaders; Mr. Schaefer likes to make the decisions himself. Thus the legislature became the crucial arena for government showdowns. Under Mr. Hughes, the General Assembly amassed considerable power to determine how programs were run and how budgetary items were spent. Under Mr. Schaefer, the Assembly has grudgingly given back some of this power, though the tug-of-war persists.

It is ironic that Mr. Schaefer begins the new decade in much the same posture as Mr. Hughes ten years ago. Back in 1980, Governor Hughes delivered a budget message that could easily be spoken by Mr. Schaefer next month: He complained that "gloomy economic forecasts and worldwide uncertainties" make budget forecasting perilous.

Revenue "falls far short of the money needed to fund all program expansions sought by state agencies and to launch the entire gamut of new services desired by a number of departments." The best he could do was "help finance the essential growth of services, a limited number of new programs" — and avoid raising sales or income taxes.

What were the priorities of 1980? The big item was money "to help the state improve prison facilities sorely neglected in previous years" plus build two new prisons. Health care "continues to be one of the state's fastest growing expenses" — requiring a spending increase of 11 percent. Local governments received an extra $56 million for community colleges, education and police. And $9 million was set aside "to save the Peabody Institute."

Ten years later, we are spending even more money to build additional prisons, watching health-care costs soar faster than ever, diverting ever-more money into local aid programs mandated by state law and devising yet another package to save the Peabody Institute.

Moreover, Mr. Schaefer is echoing the earlier Hughes complaints about revenues being insufficient to meet pressing needs while cautious economic forecasts have cut into the money available for programs. The best he can hope to achieve is modest expansion of existing programs, a few innovations — and no big tax hikes. Sounds familiar, doesn't it?

The cast of characters has changed. When Governor Hughes was addressing the 1980 legislature, his lieutenant governor was Sam Bogley, who has disappeared from public view; the attorney general was Stephen Sachs; the Senate president was James Clark; the House speaker was Benjamin Cardin, and the state treasurer was William S. James.

The one constant has been Comptroller Louis L. Goldstein. While he is a corny and unabashed showman, Mr. Goldstein is also a formidable fiscal conservative. His caution in predicting future tax revenue forced both governors to reduce their revenue estimates, much to their annoyance. But Mr. Goldstein's approach has worked over the years. Yes, it can lead to giant surpluses when the comptroller's forecasts are too timid; but in times of economic weakness, his forecasts have saved the state.

General Assembly leaders have tended to side with Mr. Goldstein. They have been wary of large spending proposals and have acted as a brake on gubernatorial ambitions that may be too grandiose.

The one blot on the decade was the savings-and-loan scandal, which posed a major threat. Had a panic developed, it could have engulfed the nation's wobbly S&Ls. But Mr. Hughes and legislative leaders stepped in quickly with $100 million of state money to quell the run.

After the Agnew and Mandel disgraces of the 1970s, the 1980s were mild by comparison. A few pols went to jail, but nothing big-time. Overall, it was an honest decade for Maryland with sound government emanating from the State House. That's about all voters can hope for or expect.

Harry Hughes practices law in Baltimore.

Schaefer Feels the Beat of Time

January 14, 1990

He wears his heart on his sleeve, which is one reason William Donald Schaefer is such a popular politician. He lets you know what he is thinking and feeling. What you see and hear is definitely what you get.

Never was that truer than Thursday in the State House, when Governor Schaefer delivered his annual State of the State address. From the outset, his inner soul was on display.

"This has not been the happiest of occasions in the last couple of weeks," he began. " I get somewhat sad and depressed." Many of his longtime political friends have died in recent months — Irvin Kovens, his political godfather; Judge Sol Liss; former Councilman Henry Hergenroeder Sr., and Councilman William J. Myers, his biggest cheerleader. The last two men died a week ago Friday and Mr. Schaefer mourned them at their funerals a few days later.

This tells us something about what is really important in life, the governor informed his attentive audience. "All of us are going to walk that road."

In his elliptical way, Mr. Schaefer was attempting to share his personal ruminations about life and death with these legislators, though this is the one group he has had the most trouble dealing with in his professional life. He is 68 years old and devoting a great deal of thought these days to his own mortality. Time, or the lack of it, is on his mind.

"There's one syndrome that I really hate: 'There's no hurry. Let's take our time.'" As he kept repeating throughout his speech, he feels there is precious little time left. If we want to accomplish anything, we have to do it — and DO IT NOW!

Thus the Schaefer administration's slogan takes on greater urgency. He wants *all* his ideas and programs in place before he leaves the governor's office for good. That gives him five more years, barring an act of God or a

Republican miracle of biblical proportions in November. And to Mr. Schaefer, five years is a short time frame to accomplish all he has on his mind.

Yet those blasted senators and delegates keep blocking his programs, killing his budget requests and trying to tell him how to run state government. It's enough to make Mr. Schaefer yearn for those days when he ran Baltimore City virtually by fiat, without having to worry about interference from a toothless City Council.

So here we go again. Even though the governor bared his soul to members of the General Assembly, passionately urged them to rally behind all the good deeds he was trying to perform, legislators refused to heed the message. There will be no $29-million snack tax, House and Senate leaders decree, and those Schaefer budget initiatives still may be trimmed by as much as $50 million.

The governor preached to legislators in his speech about cooperation. But his definition of cooperation is 100-percent alignment on administration bills. That won't happen. Ever. It goes against human nature.

Yet his package of bills will be approved, with a few exceptions. His budget priorities are likely to pass the legislature, too, with a few exceptions. And his batting average, after the final gavel has been pounded, will be so high Mr. Schaefer could qualify for immediate induction into baseball's Hall of Fame. Move over, Jim Palmer.

The truth is that Mr. Schaefer is the best motivator this state has ever seen. He knows how to energize a situation. He prods and goads and prods until he gets action and then results. He is never satisfied. He always demands more.

That style works brilliantly with the bureaucracy. It works wonderfully with citizen groups. It doesn't work too well with the legislature, whose job it is to study and mull over new laws. Sometimes lawmakers conclude that inaction is the best course of action. Sometimes they opt for lengthy study. Sometimes they flat-out reject ideas they don't like. That's their job — to act as a filter for the thousands of ideas introduced as bills each year.

Mr. Schaefer's State of the State speech was more than just a revealing look inside the psyche of this fascinating man. It was a plea to legislators for understanding and compassion. From now on, they may be more sympathetic toward the governor's objectives, even when they oppose him. A kinder, gentler General Assembly? Perhaps. But a born-again General Assembly dedicated to Mr. Schaefer's "do it now" philosophy? Hardly.

Chapter 5

Never *a* Dull Moment

Rain on Schaefer's Parade

January 20, 1991

Inauguration Day is supposed to be a festive occasion. A time for celebrating a politician's successful election to office. A time for looking optimistically to the future. So why was there all that gloom in Annapolis last week?

The depressing mood Wednesday matched the downcast weather. Even William Donald Schaefer managed few smiles. What should have been a high point for him turned into another burdensome chore.

The governor's staffers sent out 16,000 invitations to the inauguration. They got few replies. Even fewer showed up. Aside from members of the governor's cabinet (who had to be there), state legislators (who had to be there), invited dignitaries and some loyal friends and admirers, the ceremony attracted a tiny audience.

True, the weather was lousy. Everyone's mind seemed to be on war and the Persian Gulf. But there were other reasons for this pervasive gloom.

No one in the legislature is looking forward to four more years of Mr. Schaefer's tension-filled reign.

He hates dealing with legislators unless he knows he can win the argument. He hates it when legislators pull surprises on him, though he has no qualms about pulling surprises on them. He insists on waging grudge warfare against legislators. He expects blanket approval of his proposals, then boils with fury when he doesn't get it.

Mr. Schaefer believes in unimpeded gubernatorial rule. He still doesn't understand why a countervailing force known as a legislature is necessary. So he resists playing the age-old legislative game of consensus. He remains a believer in the philosophy espoused by former football coach Frank Kush: "It's either my way or the highway."

Further dampening legislative and gubernatorial spirits is the state's abysmal financial situation.

Twice already the governor has chopped away at his own cherished programs to close a $423 million budget shortfall. Now more must be sacrificed to balance next year's budget. Even worse, the legislature's fiscal analyst thinks that revenue projections made just last month have already missed the mark. If that is so, legislators will be forced to cut the governor's already reduced budget by as much a $100 million just to keep the books balanced. And if House Speaker R. Clayton Mitchell Jr. insists on blocking a transfer of corporate income tax funds to the operating budget, the General Assembly's chopping block could set an all-time record of nearly $200 million.

That will be a wrenching task for legislators. It will infuriate the governor. No one relishes the day of fiscal reckoning.

In the weeks leading to Inauguration Day, Mr. Schaefer was "up and down like a yo-yo," in the words of one observer. He would bemoan his plight one moment, then turn joyful the next. He would praise legislators publicly, then curse then in private conversations. He fretted about receiving "only" 59 percent of the vote last November, then publicly thanked voters for their trust. He was not a happy man.

No wonder; the next four years could be trying times. His big plans for expanded government services and major capital improvements could be strangled by a sagging economy and an apparent message from voters of "no new taxes — cut government spending!"

Compounding his troubles, Mr. Schaefer must deal with people he doesn't fully trust.

Lieutenant Governor Melvin A. Steinberg, though he is the governor's lone effective link to the legislature, seems to spend as much time in the Schaefer doghouse as some journalists we know.

Senate President Thomas V. Mike Miller Jr. sends the governor into fits of rage when he dares to comment negatively on a Schaefer suggestion.

Speaker Mitchell has put himself in Mr. Schaefer's Hades by seeking to block action this year on tax reforms and tax increases.

And reporters! Well, these people do nothing but write "negative, negative" stories about the governor. They make him look like an ogre. Yet he has got to deal with them. It is one of his least favorite duties.

Still, Mr. Schaefer managed to deliver an inaugural speech filled with optimism and positive thoughts. He received a smattering of polite applause. He somehow stopped the rain long enough to let the sun shine through as he delivered his address.

How different from his first inaugural, when enthusiasm for the ex-mayor of Baltimore was as high as the expectations — despite the frigid temperatures. He was a hero then; now he is a known commodity. Our expectations in these recessionary times are modest. That's not Mr. Schaefer's style. He is having enormous trouble adjusting to the minimalism that voters seem to want from their leaders in the 1990s.

S---house of a Sideshow

February 17, 1991

"It takes people's minds off of the war." — William Donald Schaefer

By now, nearly everyone in Maryland has heard Governor Schaefer's scatological comment about the land east of the Chesapeake. ("How's that s---house of an Eastern Shore?") He has been condemned, defended and derided. He's been called profane, immature and a disgrace to his office.

The governor, claiming the remark was a jest aimed at a longtime friend from the shore, thinks the uproar is "one of the silliest things I have ever seen in my life."

He said he had "absolutely nothing to apologize about." Yet five days later, there he was publicly eating crow: "I made a terrible mistake... I apologize."

Welcome to the State House circus, a three-ring spectacle where an occasional sideshow has been on display since Mr. Schaefer arrived in 1987. It is part of the governor's *modus operandi*. When times get tough, it's time for a good diversion.

Mr. Schaefer is famed for his tantrums, his mood swings, his not-so-funny public jests, his quirky behavior and, above all, for his iron will to succeed.

No governor has brought such intensity to the job. His "do it now" sloganeering is part of a stubborn, driven desire to build Rome in a day.

Yet there is a human element that is often overlooked. Don Schaefer wants to be liked. He is deeply hurt when people turn against him.

Even when 60 percent of the voters endorsed him for re-election last year, the governor wondered what he did to anger the other 40 percent. He's still stewing about it. This is one politician who hates rejection.

Donald Schaefer has led a charmed life. Since 1955, he has never had a close election. He is used to dominating the political arena. That's the way it worked in Baltimore when he was mayor.

In Baltimore, his "do it now" approach brought instant results. Potholes he spotted were filled, dirty alleys he toured were cleaned and bureaucrats were hounded until they transformed the city.

This strategy doesn't work in Annapolis. The ship of state is bigger and harder to steer. The governor must share power with the legislature. He can't simply tour the state in search of potholes. "Do it now" often means "we'll get to it later."

During last year's campaign, Mr. Schaefer anticipated a second term filled with big achievements.

Then came the recession.

Now it appears the final Schaefer years will be marked by a scramble to hold things together. Maryland is deep in a fiscal hole. The bad revenue news of December and the $423 million in budget cuts are just the start. Revenue receipts remain in a free-fall. Unemployment lines are growing. The legislature is intent on making steep budget cuts.

This means painful cutbacks. And layoffs. Progress in education and social programs could be reversed. The governor may not have the cash even to fill in the potholes.

Everywhere the governor turns, there is bad news.

He is personified as the evil ogre by state workers furious over benefit cuts; groups furious over cuts in social programs; gun owners furious over the drive to ban assault weapons, and citizens furious over the governor's tax overhaul plan.

You can add Eastern Shore residents to that list. They're furious as well — apology or no apology.

Mr. Schaefer has tried to cushion the pain, but he doesn't get any credit. He frequently has backed down from controversial stands when faced with strong criticism. That hasn't removed the bitterness felt by affected constituents.

No wonder the governor is frustrated. No wonder he takes out his anger on easy targets, such as letter writers to local newspapers who have criticized him. He strikes back by sending the writers blunt responses. He upbraids local columnists that way, too.

His underlying refrain: Why don't you love me? Why don't you appreciate the good things I have done? Why are you always criticizing me?

This is not normal. Governors aren't supposed to show their emotions. They aren't supposed to fly into a rage, use profanity or mockery or apologize for mistakes. Governors are our political heroes. And heroes aren't supposed to have feet of clay.

Donald Schaefer is not your average governor. His actions are indeed abnormal — for a governor. But if you view Don Schaefer simply as a very human executive under enormous stress and constant public pressure, who wants desperately to be admired and appreciated, his actions are more understandable.

Besides, they do take people's minds off the Persian Gulf war.

Edge of the Volcano

March 10, 1991

Living on the edge of a volcano poses immense dangers. Ask Mickey Steinberg. Since 1987, he's been forced to exist close to Annapolis' most ferocious — and unpredictable — natural wonder.

Mr. Steinberg desperately wants to avoid being consumed in the increasingly fiery eruptions occurring on Mt. William Donald Schaefer. Maryland's governor is making life increasingly difficult for his lieutenant governor.

It has been a troubled marriage ever since Mr. Schaefer chose Mr. Steinberg, then Senate president, for his 1986 ticket over the apparent front runner, Delegate R. Clayton Mitchell. It was a political decision, based on the belief Mr. Steinberg's inclusion would ensure victory.

The two men have never been close. Mickey Steinberg is a consensus-seeking product of the state legislature. He understands what it takes to craft a bill that will make it through the legislative maze.

Don Schaefer, on the other hand, is a product of the Baltimore City Council. As mayor, he mastered the art of running an impoverished city through one-man rule. When it comes to dealing with an independent legislature, Mr. Schaefer — unlike Mr. Steinberg — is on foreign soil.

Mr. Schaefer trusts only those whose loyalty has been proven over the years. That does not include Mr. Steinberg, who has been fingered by Schaefer aides as siding too often with the hated legislature.

There were signs last fall that the Schaefer inner circle intended to isolate Mr. Steinberg even more in the second term. Schaefer campaign literature, for instance, made no mention of the lieutenant governor.

This led to Mr. Steinberg's first act of defiance. When the Schaefer camp set up a fund-raising arm under the Steinberg name without his permission, the lieutenant governor called it "overkill" and "arrogance" by a governor with $2 million in the bank.

"Blasphemy," cried Schaefer sycophants. It was viewed as an indication Mr. Steinberg wanted to distance himself from Mr. Schaefer in preparation for his own gubernatorial bid. Friends of Mr. Steinberg call it political self-preservation.

The governor's frequent temper tantrums have sharply diminished his popularity and effectiveness. Meanwhile, Mr. Steinberg's savvy legislative advice — he was the architect of most Schaefer triumphs in the first term — is being ignored. As a result, this year's top Schaefer initiatives are headed for defeat.

The latest break occurred when the lieutenant governor refused to accept the governor's "all or nothing" position on the Linowes tax plan. At one meeting, Mr. Steinberg pressed for a compromise.

The governor's response? No way. "I'm not letting the bastards off the hook," he told the lieutenant governor.

Mr. Steinberg, not wishing to be a part of this kamikaze flight, begged off from testifying at the hearing on the Linowes bill. "The son of a bitch took a walk," said one bitter Schaefer assistant. "He doesn't want to be associated with anything controversial because he's running for governor in 1994."

Steinberg supporters see it differently. "Mickey knows you can't bludgeon these guys in the legislature," said one Steinberg friend. "Schaefer's approach is self-defeating."

The net result: Mr. Schaefer led the administration's team himself in appearing before the legislature on the Linowes bill. It was a fruitless exercise.

Earlier in the day, the governor made his bitterness clear at a meeting with legislative leaders when he turned to his lieutenant governor and said, "Thanks, Mickey, for stabbing me in the back."

Meanwhile, the governor continues to burn his bridges, turning Delegate Timothy Maloney — a key member of the Appropriations Committee — from an ally into a puzzled detractor by his angry tirade over a modest budget cut.

Mr. Schaefer's actions also have alienated House Speaker Mitchell, who started the session on excellent terms with the governor but no longer can comprehend the governor's outbursts. "Schaefer's now out to cut Mitchell apart," said one administration official.

That leaves Mr. Schaefer with few friends in the legislature, and a growing number of disenchanted citizens.

It also leaves his lieutenant governor in a perilous predicament: The more Mickey Steinberg speaks his mind in preparation for 1994, the more he enrages Don Schaefer. But to remain silent as Mr. Schaefer lurches from one political debacle to another could also sink Mr. Steinberg's election hopes. That's the chance you take living so close to the volcano.

Mickey Steinberg, defeated in the 1994 gubernatorial Democratic primary, practices law in Baltimore.

For Schaefer, It Was a Very Bad Year

January 5, 1992

No Marylander was happier to see 1991 fade into history last week than Gov. William Donald Schaefer. No one. It was a nightmarish year for the governor, a year in which nothing went right and nearly all his dreams as chief executive were shattered.

It should have been the best of times. Mr. Schaefer was, after all, reelected in a landslide in November 1990 for a second four-year term. He planned to launch three sweeping initiatives that would stand as his crowning achievement. His ambitious plans for Maryland looked like they were about to take flight.

But it never happened.

First, Mr. Schaefer, to the surprise of his political friends and allies, went into a deep depression after the election. He was distraught that he had won only 59 percent of the general election vote. Others reminded him that experts view such a winning margin as a landslide, but he would have none of it. He complained about the 41 percent who hadn't voted for him.

Before he could emerge from his depression, the recession hit Maryland. The year was to be filled with growing budget deficits that necessitated major cuts in state programs. Eventually, local aid had to be slashed, too. A black cloud enveloped the State House and stayed there the entire year.

None of Mr. Schaefer's Big Three initiatives passed muster. His tax-reform plan, derived from the Linowes commission study, ran into such staunch opposition it never was even considered by lawmakers. His growth-control plan, derived from the Barnes commission "2020" study, met such vehement resistance from local officials that it, too, was lost. And a plan for a hefty rise in the gasoline tax foundered amid cries of "no more taxes."

That left the governor without money to improve education, to help poor subdivisions or to upgrade roads and mass-transit systems. It also left him with no plan to save the state from hodge-podge overdevelopment in the years ahead.

Compounding the Schaefer problem was the governor's penchant for venting his anger at critics.

When one individual made a gesture at him on a street corner, the governor had state troopers note her car tags and then wrote her a nasty note, proclaiming, "Your action only exceeds the ugliness of your face."

He fired back at another critic with a memo that called him "a frustrated little boy."

To those who staged an anti-Schaefer rally in front of the Governor's Mansion, Mr. Schaefer sent Christmas photographs of the protesters at the rally, all the while denying these were State Police photos. Cries of police-state intimidation were heard.

But his worst gaffe was one he claims was meant as a joke.

As he walked down the aisle of the House of Delegates to deliver his annual state of the state address, the governor stopped to shake the hand of an old friend from the Eastern Shore and said, "How's that s---house of an Eastern Shore?"

The delegate took it for an off-color bit of Scheaferesque humor; residents of the Shore viewed it otherwise. They went bonkers. They are still hopping mad.

For all this, Mr. Schaefer earned a headline in a national gossip tabloid as the nation's wackiest governor. It helped send Mr. Schaefer's popularity into a steep tailspin. It remains at embarrassingly low levels: a recent poll showed Mr. Schaefer with an astounding negative rating of 70 percent.

The governor's sensitivity to criticism, his unwillingess to compromise on issues and his resistance to sharing power with state legislators exacerbated his problems. Now he has minimal influence in the General Assembly. What was supposed to be his greatest vehicle for creating a pro-Schaefer majority, legislative redistricting, has turned out to be totally useless for that purpose. He has frittered away much of his gubernatorial power.

Added to these woes was the governor's distress over the long illness of his close companion, Hilda Mae Snoops, which turned the Governor's Mansion into a state-financed nursing home, with state troopers acting as nurses' aides.

And now, as Mr. Schaefer looks ahead to the New Year that has just begun, the outlook is far from bright. The General Assembly returns to Annapolis on Wednesday, an event that must make the governor cringe. His difficulty in running the state — and his emotional frame of mind — worsens when the House and Senate are in session.

But perhaps his most troubling enemy this year is the state's huge budget shortfall. It will force him later this month to present a fiscal plan that guts state government agencies. He will have to decimate most of the programs he helped put in place over the past five years. With legislators still apparently unwilling to raise taxes, the Draconian cuts in state agencies could prove fearful, especially for a governor who wears his heart on his sleeve.

Presiding over the dismantling of state social programs won't be easy for Mr. Schaefer, who ardently believes in the goodness that can flow from the activities of government. He'll be the one pulling the plug on "people programs" and he'll be the one blamed for hurting people in need of help.

But he has little choice, given the "no more taxes" climate and the state's deep deficit. It's a heck of a way to start 1992. Still, this year just couldn't be as bad for Mr. Schaefer as 1991. Or could it?

The Legend of Wally Appleseed

February 16, 1992

Wally Appleseed has been at it now for more than two years, preaching his "trees are good" gospel to the heathens. And he has turned many in his audience into converts.

During this brief span of time, more than 2.5 million baby trees have been planted in Maryland under his guidance, an achievement that only future generations will fully appreciate.

The best part is that Wally Appleseed has accomplished this without bankrupting the public coffers. In fact, he is a prime example of how some government programs can be run inexpensively and yet still produce tremendous results.

Tremendous is the operative word, or rather "Tree-mendous" as the program is officially known in typical Schaefer-hype. It has spent $250,000 in two years but little has been wasted on staff salaries. (The entire staff consists of Wally Appleseed and a secretary.)

This works out to 10 trees planted in Maryland for every dollar spent. As word of the program spreads, its popularity is likely to soar, and its cost-to-value ratio will look even better.

Wally Appleseed, as you may have surmised by now, is Walter S. Orlinsky, the one-time *Wunderkind* and *enfant terrible* of Baltimore City politics. His years as council president were tumultuous. He feuded constantly with then-Mayor William Donald Schaefer, who finally cut off all diplomatic relations. (Melvin Steinberg, take note.)

Eventually, a once-promising political career self-destructed when a bored and embittered Mr. Orlinsky took a bribe to influence the award of a city contract.

But this tale has a happy ending. Once out of jail, Mr. Orlinsky decided to seek redemption. He wanted to make a contribution to society. He wanted to clear his name.

With the assent of now-Governor Schaefer, Mr. Orlinksy was hired by an old Bolton Hill-Charles Village political ally, Natural Resources Secretary Torrey C. Brown, as Maryland's first official tree-preacher. The gamble has paid off. Mr. Orlinsky, the inveterate city boy, is now a walking advocate for the glories of nature and tree-planting.

Want to help clean up the bay, or suck up some of the state's smog or reduce hot summer temperatures a bit? Plant a tree.

Or better yet, join the "buy a tree" program, modeled after the Jewish National Fund's trees-for-Israel campaign. For just $12, a six-inch tree will be planted in the honoree's name in the subdivision of your choice.

Civic groups can get involved, such as the Friends of Druid Hill, which already has planted 60 or 70 seedlings under a program to give parks the gift of trees. The Green Guerilla Army of volunteers, a cadre of volunteers, plants trees and takes care of them. The Greening of Dundalk buys and supervises the planting of trees in its community. Winchester Homes agreed to donate one million seedlings; Hardees gave 300,000 seedlings last year.

Highways offer an especially enticing opportunity for Wally Appleseed. Six hundred children from a private school in Annapolis held a plant-a-thon last year to place 14,000 seedlings on a tract of weeded highway land.

Highway cloverleafs can be turned into groves of trees that would be ideal to absorb some of the nearby automotive pollution and also act as sound barriers for adjoining housing developments.

But there's a catch: bureaucrats don't like trees near their roads. It makes it tough to mow the grass.

Look at what happened at Black Marsh State Park in Eastern Baltimore County. Volunteers planted 300 ash, oak and dogwood seedlings only to have the area mowed down by state maintenance workers. Lawn mowing, it turns out, is responsible for the largest number of seedling deaths in the program.

"Culturally, planting trees the natural way — letting trees grow and eventually choking off the grass naturally as they grow taller — is hard for us to deal with," Mr. Orlinsky admits.

Historically, most of Maryland has been shorn of its trees every 200 years or so, according to Mr. Orlinsky. Between Colonial times and the Civil War, 90 percent of the state's land was cleared. By the end of World War II, more than 40 percent of those trees had been restored through re-plantings.

But since the 1950s and the onslaught of suburban development, urban sprawl and continuing population growth, we have been losing more and more trees every year.

Wally Orlinsky's objective is to reverse that trend. He's off to a good start. "My job is to do it without any money," he said. That's a bit of hyperbole, but not by much. Johnny Appleseed, who spent 50 years spreading seeds and seedlings throughout the Ohio Valley and into the Midwest, would be proud of him.

Wally Orlinsky's state job was eliminated by Governor Glendening. He now keeps active in various ways in Baltimore.

McGuirk's Last Student Passes His Exam

April 26, 1992

Right about now, Harry McGuirk is probably looking down from that Great Political Clubhouse in the sky and nodding his approval. His last student has started to learn some of the lessons the old South Baltimore wizard tried to impart.

It makes no difference that William Donald Schaefer is four years older than was Mr. McGuirk, who died suddenly last week. Harry was the more mature and more skilled legislative operative. But then, Harry was a sage voice on the legislative scene long before his hair turned so angelic white that a reporter once likened it to meringue.

Harry McGuirk: acknowledged master of the legislative process in Annapolis and at City Hall. He knew more about drafting a bill, amending a bill and getting a bill passed than any current member of the General Assembly. Tales of his brilliance abound. He's been a legend in State House hallways for two decades.

He seemed to flounder, though, in imparting his wisdom to Governor Schaefer. Though Mr. McGuirk was a gubernatorial aide for four years, he had only limited success getting the governor to heed his advice.

Mr. McGuirk understood intuitively how legislatures worked. He understood the importance of a governor acting as a consensus-builder and leader. The governor should be the one giving lawmakers a sense of focus while he slowly builds a majority coalition on key issues.

Coalition-building, though, isn't this governor's forte. It takes time and infinite patience and an enormous amount of flexibility. That's not Don Schaefer's style. Occasionally, he would follow the McGuirk pattern, but soon the lessons would be forgotten as Mr. Schaefer reignited old feuds with the legislature.

That pattern changed abruptly at the tail end of this past General Assembly session. Donald Schaefer started acting like a governor. Instead of fighting with the legislature, he identified key issues where he and a House-Senate alliance saw eye to eye. They then worked in unison to push through a controversial budget and tax package.

It was a virtuoso performance, worthy of a Marvin Mandel or a Harry McGuirk. First, the governor put his foot down when House members, under pressure from tobacco lobbyist Bruce Bereano, sought to shelve any tobacco tax increase.

At one meeting, the governor warned House leaders that if they wanted to do Mr. Bereano's bidding, fine, but he was concerned about stopping kids from smoking and reducing Maryland's high cancer rate. Either pass his 20-cent tax hike on cigarettes or the governor said he'd veto the entire tax package.

His threat worked. So did the governor's quiet discussions with legislative leaders to find ways out of their last-minute differences. And then, to send just the right message for future legislatures, Mr. Schaefer rewarded his allies with $35 million in school construction projects for their home districts.

Opponents cried foul. They know better. It was simply an exercise in old-fashioned politics — to the victors belong the spoils. Harry McGuirk knew how this rule works. And now, Governor Schaefer was applying the rule superbly.

At last, Mr. Schaefer had become an integral part of the legislative scene. He had effectively used resources at his disposal. And he had done so with enough sophistication and force to win a major victory.

This holds great promise. Perhaps Mr. Schaefer won't be a lame duck governor after all. A powerful coalition emerged. It consists of House Speaker R. Clayton Mitchell and his large leadership contingent, the suburban delegations from Prince George's and Montgomery Counties and politicians from Baltimore City. Put them together with a governor who knows how to reward his allies, and the Schaefer administration's future could be rosy.

What a pity Harry McGuirk won't be around to see it. He'd be in his element. Not only did he add color and an aura of mystery to the Annapolis scene (the constant refrain was, "What's Harry up to?"), he knew how to make good legislation better and a poorly drafted bill passible.

Dozens of legislators still tell stories of Harry McGuirk going out of his way to help them when they were rookie lawmakers. He'd offer to re-shape a bill or re-word a mangled section so it would be acceptable.

If a bill reached the floor in a form that threatened passage, Mr. McGuirk would be there to offer revisions to make it viable.

He served as a one-man backstop, spotting minute but fatal flaws. On one occasion in the early 1970s, he stunned colleagues by finding a misplaced comma in a 200-page re-codification bill — a dry, technical document that reorganized and updated the Annotated Code. As it turned out, the comma totally changed existing law. It was a typical McGuirk discovery that had escaped everybody else's attention.

Governor Schaefer will miss Harry McGuirk. Yet perhaps it was the proper time for Harry to exit *sine die*. The governor seems to have mastered some of the master's teachings. Now if only the legislature can find another Harry McGuirk, maybe the quagmire known as the General Assembly will gets its act together, too.

Voice of the People Heard for a Price

June 14, 1992

Pssst! Wanna hire a bigtime lobbyist? Here's the secret: come up with an average of $13,169 and one of Maryland's top five influence-peddlers in Annapolis is yours. C.O.D., of course.

This has been a banner year for Maryland lobbyists. There may be a prolonged recession out there, but for the persistent persuaders of the State House, these are boom times.

Talk about making a living wage! These guys and gals are raking in the cash. The top five lobbyists alone received payments of $2.1 million from their 163 clients for just six months' worth of work.

Clearly, this is a growth industry. Don't tell your kids to grow up to be cowboys, or even doctors. Tell them to be lobbyists.

The pay can't be beat. You get to schmooze with the powerful and enjoy a life of luxury during the General Assembly session. The rest of the year can be spent aboard your newly purchased yacht, since nothing much happens in Annapolis between June and January.

What if your group or cause cannot afford $13,000 to hire a Top Gun? Well, you're out of luck. It takes money to grease the wheels of democracy. Those who have it generally get their way. Those who aren't well-endowed learn a lesson in the workings of a free-market legislature.

Is Annapolis for sale? It looks that way. Today, you have to buy influence. And legislators often are just as culpable as the lobbyists themselves. Many lawmakers expect to be wined and dined. During the 90-day legislative session, these solons enjoy the high life. The parties are smashing. Gourmet dining, with the lobbyist picking up the tab, is *de rigueur*. Doing favors for legislators is part of a lobbyist's job.

Even when the General Assembly isn't in session, legislators have their hands out. Lobbyists are expected to contribute handsomely to scores of fundraisers. The amounts being raised are enormous. How much of this money is

used indirectly to enhance a legislator's standard of living is a matter of speculation. But lobbyists feel the heat when the solicitations arrive in the mail. Delegate Casper Taylor recently held a golf tournament in Western Maryland. The place was crawling with lobbyists. Why? Because Mr. Taylor chairs the Economic Matters Committee, which handles most business-related bills. Two Baltimore lobbyists, though they have scant regard for Mr. Taylor, showed up anyway and paid for hundreds of dollars worth of tickets. The rationale? "We'd better go. He's the chairman."

There are numerous methods for winning over delegates and senators. One way is to develop a close, personal relationship greased by moola. For instance, top lobbyist Bruce Bereano is eager to take legislators to sports events — the best seats at Oriole Park or the Capital Centre or even seats to the Super Bowl. Mr. Bereano also knows when to give a vulnerable legislator a helping hand. He's involved in raising money for Delegate Tony Fulton's Legal Defense Fund to pay expenses related to charges that he had violated election laws in disbursing campaign funds. This helps Mr. Bereano's clients when it comes time for Mr. Fulton to cast votes on bills of interest to the lobbyist.

Health care has become an especially lucrative topic for lobbyists. This past General Assembly session, health-related groups paid $1.3 million to gain representation — and influence. Gerard E. Evans' law firm took in $400,000 from 12 health groups, with Mr. Evans alone amassing a quarter-million dollars. You've got to have some kind of influence to amass that kind of payment.

Horse-racing, too, meant big bucks for lobbyists: $280,000. This was the year for off-track betting, and the wallets of concerned groups were generously opened to win passage. And one company that had no hot and burning issue in the legislature this year, GTECH, the state's lottery contractor, still opted to display its gratitude for the good work of Mr. Bereano and his sometime sidekick, Marvin Mandel. The company paid the duo $96,000. Imagine how much the twosome would have netted had this been a busy year for their client in Annapolis.

There's nothing illegal in all this. But that doesn't make it right. Fees paid to lobbyists are bordering on the obscene. The willingness of legislators to be lavished with perks is also obscene. Economic interest groups are flocking to Annapolis either to defend or expand their turf for financial gain. Each group is eager to pay handsomely for hiring these influence peddlers.

You can't ban lobbyists from the legislature. Every individual and every group has a legitimate right to be heard. And because so many legislators are too lazy to do their own homework on issues, lobbyists play an important educational role.

Old-fashioned lobbyists, like James J. Doyle, still rely heavily on the persuasiveness of their arguments. But younger lobbyists have modeled themselves after Mr. Bereano, who uses his personal connections to legislators and government leaders to gain leverage.

Money talks these days in Annapolis. That's a sad fact of life. It's also one of the key reasons Marylanders are fed up with elected leaders. Lobbyists play too big a role in State House affairs. The people know it, even if legislators don't.

William S. James: Civility and Selflessness

April 25, 1993

An important bit of Maryland passed from our midst the other day when William S. James died at age 79. He looms large in State House history, a civilizing influence in a capital dominated by political heathens.

His public career spanned 43 years. For much of the 1960s, 1970s and 1980s, he played a major role in shaping state government's achievements. But in the late '80s and '90s, he was a forgotten figure. Not coincidentally, the Annapolis scene deteriorated badly after his humiliating rejection as state treasurer in 1987. His calming, intellectual influence has been sorely missed.

Bill James was an old-fashioned man, almost Victorian in his manners and political etiquette. At first meeting him, you'd never assume that he was a leader: He had a sing-song, high-pitched voice and a withered arm. It was his mental powers that impressed — and his high sense of ethical standards. By sheer force of intellectual power, he imposed gentility and civility on the state Senate.

Mr. James' Senate was gentlemanly. Debates were informative and high-toned. Angry diatribes and personal arguments weren't tolerated. Everyone abided by the rules of parliamentary conduct — and no one knew the details better than the acknowledged parliamentary and constitutional expert, Bill James.

Annapolis lacks this sort of intellectual and institutional memory. There's little respect for the details of state law and procedures any more. This is the what's-in-it-for-my-political-career generation of office holders. Doing good deeds for the state just is not of primary concern.

For the politicians of Mr. James' era, the reverse held sway. His list of contributions is long, yet little of it helped him with voters back home. That did not matter. What did matter was doing the right thing.

He was Mr. Environment long before that term had positive connotations. He put his prestige on the line for land-use controls, for farmland preservation, for the Maryland Environmental Service, for Program Open Space. He was a major backer of Baltimore City. He was a ceaseless booster of education.

"I rate as my greatest achievement," he wrote in a hand-written letter after his forced retirement from government, "the drafting and sponsoring with [Sen.] Mary Nock [of Salisbury] the legislation upon which the Maryland community college system is founded." What modern-day senator can claim an accomplishment of such magnitude?

The State House misses Bill James. Had he been presiding over the Senate this past session, there never would have been the embarrassing John Arnick episode: Mr. James would have been appalled by charges of improper and sexist comments. His horror of someone with such an attitude on the bench would have ended that fiasco.

Nor would there have been the continuing Senate embarrassment over legislative scholarships. Mr. James detested these patronage awards and nearly got them outlawed in the early 1970s. He'd have finished the job long before now.

Mr. James spent 20 years as a senator, the last 12 as president of the chamber. He presided over the upper chamber longer than anyone else had in Senate history. He left after winning appointment as state treasurer, the position from which he got the boot at the behest of Gov. William Donald Schaefer in 1987. What an ignominious way to go for such a mannered gentleman. He never understood why the governor would treat him so rudely.

"In brief," Mr. James wrote, "at considerable political risk, I was always a friend of Baltimore City, who deserved Don Schaefer's support for re-election as Treasurer. However, he did not reply to my request for an appointment, and he was very discourteous upon the several times I saw him in the State House. His ingratitude and his incivility, not only to me, but to Governor [Harry] Hughes, astonished me."

So the man who represented the highest traditions of public service, who embodied the best qualities of the citizen-legislator, left Annapolis. For the first time in 43 years, Bill James returned to his Havre de Grace farm without a title attached to his name, but with his outlook on life still firmly rooted.

"In all probability," he wrote in 1987, "defeat may be a good thing for me personally. I live in a paradise of natural beauty, which I have protected by giving the state an environmental easement. I never tire of watching the geese and other wild creatures. I have a small office in Bel Air, which keeps me in touch with the legal profession. My civic activities include several charitable and educational institutions. I am blessed with good health, my days will be full, and my interest in public affairs continues. When all else fails, I have my books and *The Sun* to read."

Now he is dead. He was once asked about his ultimate goal in life. His response was "that the greatest achievement in a democracy is to be remembered as a good citizen."

Bill James fulfilled this goal remarkably well. He was, indeed, a good citizen — among the very best this state has had in the last half of the 20th century.

Labor's Shrinking Power: A Case Study

September 5, 1993

As Labor Day approaches, the state of organized labor remains in decline. Ever since the high point in 1955, when one-third of the American work force held union cards, labor organizations have been shrinking. The unionized figure now stands at about 16 percent of U.S. non-agricultural workers. But don't blame it all on the unions. Blame much of it on societal changes. Look at what has happened, for instance, in Annapolis during the past quarter-century.

Back in 1968, labor was king in the State House. Union leaders would hand out a sheet to their loyal delegates and senators on which way to vote on that week's bills. These orders were followed. When a labor lobbyist testified before a committee, his disapproval could often kill a measure.

In contrast, business interests had no unified voice in the hallways of Annapolis. The state Chamber of Commerce that had just been formed was actually an adjunct of the Baltimore C. of C. It didn't even have its own office in the state capital. Business representatives had little impact on legislation.

But now the reverse is true: The Maryland Chamber of Commerce is booming with influence and prestige; labor unions no longer exert much power in Annapolis. Few lawmakers toe the union line on bills, but hordes of them heed the advice on bills from the chamber's savvy band of lobbyists. The chamber is respected; the unions are tolerated.

What has happened? Labor's traditional source of clout in the legislature — industrial, blue-collar neighborhoods in the Baltimore area — has lost population, and thus holds far fewer seats in the General Assembly. Big unionized work forces have shrunk dramatically — Bethlehem Steel employed more than 20,000 workers a quarter-century ago; now that number is down to 8,000. Population has shifted to the suburbs from the traditionally unionized city. The suburbs dominate the legislature and their representatives tend to be better educated, more business-wise and more independent. Business has done a good job of educating the public. Twenty-five years ago, no one used the term "economic development." It never occurred to anyone that imposing onerous requirements on companies or hiking unemployment insurance and workers' compensation expenses could actually harm workers by forcing businesses to cut back on staffing or leave the state entirely.

It wasn't until the end of the 1970s that economic development became a hot subject for political discussion. Ever since then, there has been a growing recognition that developing a good business climate is often more important for workers than anything else the state can do.

And certainly the general public is more aware of business and finance matters these days.

Look at the amount of space devoted to business news in *The Sun*. Look at the growing popularity of business newspapers and specialty finance magazines.

And look at the way public officials react when a business opportunity is threatened or an existing business is endangered: They rush to the rescue.

It has become good politics to preach economic development and to adopt the mantra, "what's good for business is good for my re-election."

Expanding business opportunities in the suburbs have meant prosperity: lots of new, high-paying jobs; lots of disposable income; lots of new home-building and a higher standard of living. For proof, look to Montgomery County and Howard County.

In the State House, the Chamber of Commerce has learned the art of coalition-building. No longer is business focused on a couple of issues like workers' comp and unemployment insurance.

The chamber is taking positions on environmental bills, consumer bills, even good-government bills. And not always in opposition.

Today, the chamber's lobbyists usually seek a middle ground. Last session, for instance, the chamber played an important role in shaping portions of the landmark health-care reform bill and then getting the votes necessary for passage. It even has formed a coalition with labor on health-care matters.

That bridge-building approach seems to be working well for business. The state chamber has grown from 241 member groups in 1971 to more than 1,500, and from a budget of $48,000 to $1.7 million. Its influence is clearly on the rise.

As for labor, it won't be a happy celebration tomorrow for local advocates of unionism. For them, the situation in the State House, and in Maryland, isn't very cheery.

Maryland Takes a Gamble (and Another)

October 3, 1993

What has William Donald Schaefer wrought? Will he be remembered as "the Gambling Governor"?

The man who brought slot machines back to Maryland? Who gave us off-track betting parlors, Lotto, Keno, El Gordo, lottery vending machines? Will his final present to the state be riverboat gambling and Indian casinos?

Late in his final term as governor, Mr. Schaefer is starting to realize that once you let gambling get a foot in the door, it is nearly impossible to ever close that door again.

He also finds himself in the contradictory position of trying to boost one kind of government-sanctioned gambling while seeking to crack down on other forms of gambling.

Two factors are at work here: Mr. Schaefer's eagerness to do good deeds for friendly citizens and his desire to come up with more money on which to complete some of his ambitious programs.

The first factor is best illustrated by the fight over slot machines. Non-profit groups on the Eastern Shore, such as the Elks, Moose and veterans groups, urged Mr. Schaefer — then a candidate for governor — to let them bring back a handful of slot machines. The idea was that money raised would flow back into the community.

Candidate Schaefer bought the idea. It was a painless way to help Shore communities.

He signed the measure in 1987. Since then, Eastern Shore officials and non-profit leaders "broke faith with me," according to the governor. The situation is out of control.

There is virtually no policing of the slots revenue; slot machines are entering the state and then disappearing; there is an on-going probe of Eastern Shore sheriffs and their close ties to slots operators.

A total of $32 million in slots activity was reported last year; no one knows how much additional money is unaccounted for. And half of the reported profits are being pumped back into the sponsoring organizations, making them fat and happy. But don't try to make these groups responsible for their actions. They respond angrily to attempts to police their activities. Their resident defender in Annapolis, Senator Walter Baker of Cecil Country, has the power to block any reform legislation. He still says there's no hanky-panky going on, though State Police know otherwise.

The governor now recognizes there is, indeed, plenty of mischief and even some criminality, but he is powerless to do anything about it.

The same holds true in Prince George's County, where casino-night gambling for charity has become big business, so big that politicians cower at the thought of reining-in the non-profit groups. Skimming of profits is widespread, few controls exist, profits are being diverted into non-charitable purchases, and professional gambling operators are active in these $20-million-a-year enterprises.

It's a mess, but state government's sanctioning of other forms of gambling makes it difficult to get tough in Prince George's County. (The situation in that jurisdiction is not really Mr. Schaefer's doing; it could, though, become a campaign headache for P.G. County Executive Parris N. Glendening, who has failed to clamp down on the casino gambling and is a leading candidate for governor.)

While bemoaning the abuses of gambling cropping up in Maryland, Mr. Schaefer simultaneously has urged lottery officials to improve sales of their lagging Keno game. He needs the extra money to boost the size of his final budget. That also could lead to his embracing a bill legalizing riverboat casino gambling.

Not far behind is the Indian casino gambling issue.

Mr. Schaefer clearly adores big economic development projects, and the group representing this state's Piscataway Indians in Southern Maryland is promising a giant development project — a huge casino, race track, hotel, amusement park and marina complex that could employ 30,000 people. It's just the kind of BIG project Mr. Schaefer loves. All he's got to do is say "yes" to the Piscataway casino.

Don't count on it. Mr. Schaefer does not want to be remembered chiefly as the governor who turned gambling loose throughout Maryland.

But what about the next governor? While Mr. Glendening says he's adamantly opposed to casino gambling of this sort (as opposed to the casinos already operating in his own county now), other potential governors aren't flat-out against the idea, not when it could mean hundreds of millions of dollars in new state tax revenues and jobs.

The gambling genie is out of the bottle. Sadly, state and local politicians don't have the gumption or even the desire to put the cork back in place.

Man in the Mirror Said, 'Time to Go'

November 21, 1993

Poor Clay Mitchell. Even on the day he suddenly announced his resignation from the second-most powerful post in Annapolis, he couldn't grab the headlines. He was aced out by the announcement of Maryland's $117 million unpaid bill to Blue Cross.

That's the way it seemed to go for the Eastern Shoreman. He never felt he got the respect he deserved during seven years as speaker of the House of Delegates. Only his problems made the headlines. His successes were barely noted.

Mr. Mitchell has a thinner skin than most politicians. He never fully adjusted to the constant pressure and hammering that a legislative leader takes. His shouting matches with the governor (and then their kiss-and-make-up sessions), his disputes with Senate President Thomas V. Mike Miller, the state prosecutor's probe of his real-estate dealings, the hand-holding a speaker does to appease 140 delegates, the constant lobbying to line up votes — it all took a toll.

At the age of 57, Roy Clayton Mitchell Jr. decided he couldn't take it any more.

"I was shaving in the mirror several weeks ago, and I looked at myself and said, 'Hey, you've just got to get out.'"

He felt he no longer had a private life, that he was being consumed by an ostensible part-time job that was really a full-time vocation. "It was tough trying to lead a dual life any more. It was crushing in on me."

"I dreaded going down on Tuesdays" to Annapolis for committee meetings in the off-session, he admitted. "I kept finding excuses for not going down."

So he gave up what looked like a bright political future. He was an odds-on favorite to wind up as the state's next treasurer. But he couldn't even bear the thought of another difficult General Assembly session next year, carrying the water for a governor who has minimal influence in the legislature.

We may not have heard the last of R. Clayton Mitchell, though. He now is a prime candidate for lieutenant governor next year. If the right gubernatorial contender makes the right offer, who knows? By then, Mr. Mitchell may have recharged his internal engines and be looking around for a new challenge. Then again, he may be content with playing grandpa, working at his Radio Shack store near the Bay Bridge and being recognized as an elder statesman on the Eastern Shore.

As for the House of Delegates, "everyone will do fine," he said.

And sure enough, within days of Mr. Mitchell's resignation announcement, a new House leader emerged. It was, though, a bizarre twist that opened the door for Delegate Casper R. Taylor of Cumberland to fulfill his longtime ambition to sit in the speaker's chair.

When Mr. Mitchell called in his leadership group to announce he was stepping down, he suggested that they select the speaker pro tem, Gary Alexander, for the next session. Mr. Alexander, who represents Prince George's County, isn't running for re-election. He seemed the perfect compromise.

That night, committee chairmen polled their panel members and found that they, too, favored Mr. Alexander. But Mr. Taylor refused to reveal his own committee's vote count. He made it clear he was running for speaker himself.

To everyone's surprise, Mr. Alexander suddenly announced he would not oppose Mr. Taylor's bid. He said he had no stomach for a fight and no reason to run against his friend, Cas Taylor. Simply by showing his willingness to fight for the job, Casper Taylor won.

Whatever the reason for this highly unusual scenario, it probably saved House members a year or more of divisive regional warfare. There was no logical successor to Mr. Mitchell. But there were a number of potential candidates. All had major flaws.

Nancy Kopp of Montgomery County had made enemies by trying to oust Mr. Mitchell last year. Tim Maloney of Prince George's County hails from the same county as the Senate president. Howard "Pete" Rawlings of Baltimore hasn't been in good health and would prefer a run for speaker after the election. Paul Weisengoff of the city wants the job but is viewed as a voice from the past. Ron Guns of Cecil County and Bruce Poole of Washington County weren't viewed as experienced heavyweights.

Only Cas Taylor has been actively maneuvering to become speaker. As a rural delegate, he was acceptable to both urban and suburban factions, as well as to the Washington and Baltimore factions.

Though he is viewed as too cozy with business lobbyists, Mr. Taylor did a masterful job earlier this year pushing through landmark health-care reform. If he takes over as House speaker in January, he would gain a year's head start on potential foes for the post.

But given the ambitions of some of his rivals, and the vast changes in the legislature following the 1994 elections in re-drawn districts, Mr. Taylor may have to wage another fight 12 months from now to hold onto his prize.

Cas Taylor still serves as speaker of the House of Delegates.

A High-flying Operator Falls to Earth

December 4, 1994

Shed no tears for Bruce Bereano. He earned his reputation as a super-lobbyist by living on the edge. Sooner or later, he was bound to fall off.

Test pilots have a term for such behavior — "pushing the envelope." Pilots force their experimental aircraft to fly as high and as fast as possible, pushing the machines to exceed prior levels of performance. Of course, there's always the chance a pilot can push too hard and wind up crashing.

That's what happened to Mr. Bereano. Having lived on the edge so long, having pushed the envelope of lobbyist influence so dramatically over the past decade, having achieved wealth, success and enormous prestige among politicians, he felt invincible. Brashness turned to arrogance. He prided himself in taking lobbying to new, creative levels without breaking the law.

But he continued to steer perilously close to disaster.

He finally got tripped up when federal investigators came across a suspicious pattern of campaign contributions to state legislators from his office workers and relatives. Digging deeper, prosecutors uncovered an illegal scheme to defraud Mr. Bereano's clients, with the lobbyist's parents, ex-wife, children and office workers serving as fronts to hide wrong-doing.

Still, the always-clever lobbyist almost beat the rap. The federal judge trying the case said it was "thin." He nearly threw it out of court. But once the case went to the jury, Mr. Bereano's fate was sealed. Ordinary people were presented with a case of a powerful, wealthy lobbyist using relatives and employees for his own advantage to evade the law. It was the type of behavior the jurors would not condone in their own lives. They refused to condone Mr. Bereano's behavior, either.

Even the timely amnesia of a key Bereano employee — who might face criminal charges herself — couldn't save him. The jury saw through her faulty memory and concluded that Mr. Bereano was manipulating people and campaign contributions to an extent that could not be tolerated. Still, we have not seen the last of Bruce Bereano. Not yet, anyway. His pride alone will drive him to maintain his lobbying practice during the next General Assembly session. But then, the lobbying profession in Annapolis already has its share of suspect operatives, including an ex-felon and a fellow twice charged with drug violations.

What a tawdry situation. No wonder the public has such a low opinion of politicians and lobbyists. For years, the growing power of lobbyists has threatened to undermine the integrity of the legislative process. And for years, lawmakers resisted a crackdown. Too many of them fell prey to the Bereanos of the State House, who ingratiate themselves with lawmakers to such an extent that a *quid pro quo* is inevitable.

An old saying reminds that there's no such thing as a free lunch. And yet there are dozens and dozens of legislators who still believe you can get something for nothing, that all the gifts and free tickets and free gourmet meals and all the booze they can consume and all that help solving their personal and business problems comes without strings.

Lobbyists hone in on the weaknesses of legislators, especially those who like to live the good life in Annapolis for 90 days each year, who enjoy being treated like VIPs, who revel in the skybox tickets, Streisand tickets and Superbowl tickets. Is there a price to be paid? You'd better believe it. No wonder some lobbyists quietly brag about controlling the votes of enough legislators to kill or pass certain bills.

It wasn't always this way. There was a time when a lobbyist would simply show up at a hearing and present a well-reasoned case on behalf of a client. Some legislators got an occasional good meal, but that was about the extent of the extracurricular activities.

Then came Bruce Bereano, with contacts developed while working for two Senate presidents. He spent a fortune influencing legislators. He became their best friend and counselor. He'd do anything.

He re-wrote the book on funding political campaigns. He bundled contributions from his 50 or more clients, then got other lobbyists to do the same. Pretty soon, legislators were deeply indebted to lobbyists for their campaign money. They came to expect this as part of the *quid pro quo*.

Mr. Bereano also plowed new ground in administrative lobbying, burrowing into the Schaefer administration to "break the egg," as he put it, and win the hugely lucrative lottery contract for his client. He followed up with another coup in the controversial no-bid Keno contract. He showed that any government decision, be it executive or legislative, can be influenced by strong, savvy lobbying. He broadened the base for his profession by a country mile.

Now, though, the new terrain Mr. Bereano helped explore and discover is being seized by his competitors.

Like hungry vultures, they are eyeing his client list as he tries to hang onto his customers tenaciously while awaiting sentencing in April on eight counts of mail fraud. The latest big-money game is casino-gambling. Lobbyists are scrambling to sign up clients.

Bruce Bereano won't be among the lobbyists stalking this fascinating new prey. He's fighting to overturn the verdict and stay out of prison. His legacy, though, is clear: He's the man who transformed lobbying in Maryland's state capital from a gentlemanly, honorable profession of modest fortune to a high-stakes, high-rewards occupation that is a booming growth industry but of low repute.

He pushed the envelope to new heights — and then crashed and burned.

Bruce Bereano's federal conviction was affirmed in August, 1998, by a three-judge federal appeals panel.

Schaefer Packs Up His Personalities

January 8, 1995

Love him or hate him, William Donald Schaefer is an unforgettable character. He is also the best news story this newspaper ever had. In just the last three years, the number of articles mentioning his full name ran to 3,719. In the previous 20 years, we probably had another 25,000 stories about him as mayor or governor. And in the 16 years before that, we had countless more articles following his city council career.

He certainly provided me with plenty of good columns. And yet I've never been able to capture the full essence of Donald Schaefer. I've known him for 24 years — he inadvertently gave me my first big break as a political reporter — without really knowing him. He's truly the man of a thousand public faces.

He has cried in public. He's laughed in public. He has shouted. He's cursed. He has wallowed in self-pity. He's pleaded for the needy. He has blustered. He's boostered. He has admonished. He's challenged.

He's played the role of a buffoon, a promoter, a motivator, a comedian, a statesman, a clear-eyed analyst of public policy and human behavior.

He's been Baltimore's greatest mayor and one of Maryland's better governors.

He's given citizens 105 percent effort and absolute personal integrity. He's given his all for "the people" and yet has been shameless in his desire to leave his name on hundreds of buildings and other sites around the state.

He has promoted himself more than any recent governor, just as he promoted himself more than any Baltimore mayor before him.

Donald Schaefer permeates my office. His angry letters to me or my superiors fill my desk drawers. Photographs of him dominate my walls.

There he is strewn with confetti and wearing a party hat at some election-night bash. Below that photo, he's closing his briefing books and preparing

to storm out of a radio debate with Attorney General Stephen H. Sachs in the 1986 campaign for governor.

Next, he's in National Guard camouflage, with aviator-style sunglasses, looking very much like his hero, George S. Patton.

Below that, he's presiding at a cabinet meeting beside Lt. Gov. Mickey Steinberg (when they were still speaking). They're wearing matching sweatshirts: His says, "Things are going. . . great!!!" Mr Steinberg's says, "If they're not. . . smile anyway."

Another photo, from an Ocean City liquor store, captures an ironic Eastern Shore sentiment (in light of all he did for that part of the state) on a roadside advertisement: "Help get rid of Schaefer/ $7.50 a case."

And there's Donald Schaefer in mayoral white shirt, dark tie and dark pants — plus a grass skirt — dancing with two bikinied Hawaiian women at War Memorial Plaza.

Finally, there's a quotation from Mr. Schaefer that serves as a reality check. It is taped to my desk. He said it at a luncheon for a group of legislators. Two of them related it to me. Out of the blue, he brought up my name and launched into a harangue about a recent column, calling me "a stupid nitwit, nothing more than a common bastard" who "doesn't do anything — just sits around like the Three Stooges."

That would deflate just about anyone's balloon.

Mr. Schaefer could be loony and wacko. Or he could be an incisive political philosopher. It was the wild mood swings that frustrated and enthralled people.

One Schaefer aide said Mr. Schaefer could humiliate and embarrass you with a brutal tongue-lashing at one meeting and sometime later lavish such praise on your work that tears would come to your eyes. Such heart-felt compliments kept aides glued to his side.

He is a totally dedicated elected leader. Public service fills every waking hour. He has sacrificed a private life to devote full time to doing good for people.

That's why it is so hard to contemplate William Donald Schaefer as Citizen Schaefer. He's been in elective office 40 years. He hasn't driven his own car in 23 years. He's had police protection all that time, too. He's got no vocation or avocation to turn to. No children or grandchildren to nurture and spoil.

One way or another, Mr. Schaefer will return to the public arena. He's filled with ideas and thoughts on how to help people. College Park may serve as a temporary locale. Professor Schaefer. He could give some astounding lectures. But he's not one to wade through piles of exams and term papers.

No, Baltimore is where his heart is. He could end up voicing his views on *The Sun's* opinion page, or even as a letters-to-the-editor writer. Journalist Schaefer.

He has volunteered to come up to the newspaper every few weeks and tell us exactly what we're doing wrong in our news and editorial sections. Ombudsman Schaefer.

He might be drafted by the next governor to serve as a roving economic-development celebrity for Maryland. He's a fabulous booster, after all. Ambassador Schaefer.

Or he could be hired by his loyal friends in Ocean City to promote the Atlantic vacation town he so adores. Huckster Schaefer.

He'll serve on prestigious boards of directors, delivering common-sense advice to management on how to get the most out of employees. Capitalist Schaefer.

But most likely, he'll find a way to remain in the political arena. He's a valuable asset dying to be tapped. If he's not tapped quickly, he could get the urge to run for office again. What's he got to lose?

There's a phrase for someone like William Donald Schaefer. *Sui generis.* In a class by himself. Unique. A figure such as the man from Edgewood Street comes along once in a lifetime. In my book, he's Marylander of the Century.

Chapter 6

The Contested Election

Campaign Cream A-Rising

May 22, 1994

It's beginning to look like two-candidate races for governor in both party primaries this year. Slowly but surely the candidates are dropping out and the cream is rising to the surface. That could greatly simplify the job for voters this summer.

In the Republican race, U.S. Representative Helen Bentley remains the heavy favorite. She's popular with the rank and file, she has a loyal base of supporters in the 2nd Congressional District and she is titular head of the state GOP. But suddenly she finds herself on the defensive.

The congresswoman has once again been trying to explain a gun-control vote, this time in opposition to banning assault weapons. Her indecision and her effort to straddle the issue certainly didn't enhance her gubernatorial image.

Now she has to fend off the aggressive thrusts of state Delegate Ellen Sauerbrey of northern Baltimore County. Ms. Sauerbrey may be a died-in-the-wool Reaganite when it comes to economics, but she wasted little time discarding Ronald Reagan's strong admonition to all Republican candidates to obey the "11th Commandment" — speak no ill of a fellow Republican.

Twice last week, she castigated Ms. Bentley for not voting in favor of radical budget cuts proposed by hard-line Republican conservatives, for not voting to trim congressional mailing privileges and for being too cozy with organized labor. She even staged an eye-catching press conference across the street from Bentley headquarters.

Sure enough, Ms. Bentley took the bait. Her staff tried to belittle the Sauerbrey charges by hand-delivering a "mudslinging kit" to the candidate during her press conference. All that did was assure Ms. Sauerbrey of heightened media coverage and breathe new life into the delegate's charges.

That's exactly what the Sauerbrey camp wanted. By going on the offensive,

Ms. Sauerbrey is setting the agenda for this Republican campaign. It's the only way she can overcome Ms. Bentley's big lead in the polls and begin to plant doubts about Ms. Bentley's loyalty to the conservative Republican cause. A third candidate, William S. Shepard, remains in the race, but he is fast becoming an afterthought. It's the Sauerbrey attacks on Ms. Bentley — and Ms. Bentley's responses — that are now the focus of attention.

Meanwhile, the Democratic primary is turning into a catch-the-leader affair. The much-anticipated entry of millionaire Stewart Bainum Jr. imploded, with the candidate developing a bad case of stage fright just as the campaign curtain was about to rise. Too bad. Mr. Bainum planned an early media blitz that would have focused on issues, not on the horse-race aspect of this election.

Parris Glendening, the academic turned Prince George's county executive, continues to gain momentum, picking up endorsements with broad promises to various interest groups.

The Glendening campaign booklet released last week, "A Vision for Maryland's Future," is a grab-bag of good-sounding ideas sure to please just about everyone. The price of this vision isn't mentioned, though. It clearly would cost far more than this state — facing a billion-dollar deficit in the next four years — can afford. So far, no one seems to have noticed.

Most Democratic eyes will be on tomorrow night's big fund-raiser in Baltimore for House Speaker Casper R. Taylor of Cumberland. Ostensibly this event is being held to give Mr. Taylor a vast kitty so he can dole out funds to loyal House colleagues this election year.

But some of Mr. Taylor's backers — egged on by Governor Schaefer — want to use this $200-a-ticket event to propel their candidate into the race for governor. That would certainly change the dynamics and present a new obstacle for Mr. Glendening.

As it is, the main challenge to a Glendening victory comes from Lieutenant Governor Mickey Steinberg. None of the other contenders has emerged as a top-tier candidate.

Mr. Steinberg could yet generate some campaign sparks if he ever brings focus to his chaotic efforts. He certainly knows the issues, he has a long record of achieving results in Annapolis and he feels passionately about many social issues.

So far, though, issues have taken a back seat in the Steinberg campaign to personality clashes and organizational problems. Meanwhile, the methodical Mr. Glendening is marching steadily forward.

There's plenty of time for Mr. Steinberg to recover lost ground. But it will take the kind of aggressiveness he has yet to display. Just as Ms. Sauerbrey seized the initiative on the GOP side, so must Mr. Steinberg start to set the agenda on the Democratic side. Otherwise, it could be an increasingly lonely and frustrating summer for Maryland's lieutenant governor.

Helen Bentley is a maritime consultant in Baltimore. Stewart Bainum Jr. continues to run several large corporations.

The Legend Just Keeps Growing

July 3, 1994

Walter G. Finch would like to be a household word. But he isn't.
He used to be one of those hardy perennials that surfaces in the political garden every election year.

The Republicans have Ross Z. Pierpont, the feisty Baltimore surgeon running for senator this year. It is his 13th campaign.

The Democrats have the lesser-known Walter Finch, a former perennial now resurfacing for the first time in 16 years to run for governor. Back in the 1960s and 1970s, the Baltimore lawyer was sure to run for Senate or Congress at every opportunity: 1966, 1968, 1970, 1974, 1976 and finally 1978 for attorney general. In that last race he finished fourth out of four candidates, more than 200,000 votes behind the primary winner, Stephen H. Sachs.

His moment of glory came in 1974, with his "walking-man" strategy. He claims to have hiked all 1,436 miles of the state's border and walked through every county seat. He won one county in that primary election — Washington — but finished a distant third, 100,000 votes behind an obscure Baltimore City Council member, Barbara A. Mikulski.

Now Walter Finch is 76 and is embarking on one more quixotic crusade. He joins the ranks of the also-rans, who show up at forums, spout their wild rhetoric and are forgotten. They aren't taken seriously. For good reason.

Here is what Mr. Finch is proposing in his campaign platform:

- "Develop state-of-the-art farming system to raise fish of all types, as well as crabs, oysters, terrapins, lobsters, wildfowl, clams, frogs and alligators and crocodiles for their leather."
- Construct an international airport on the Eastern Shore or in Western Maryland big enough to handle the largest jet aircraft of the world "and possibly space travel in the 21st century."
- "Construct the latest up-to-date and state-of-the-art 'Astro-Sphere' for

planetary study of the heavens."
- "Construct small or medium-size atomic-energy plants on the Eastern Shore and in Western Maryland."
- "Construct a two-lane double-decker bridge or a four-lane bridge across the northern Chesapeake Bay and/or an underwater tunnel to the Eastern Shore."
- "Call a Constitutional Convention in 1996 to rewrite, clarify and revise the present antiquated State Constitution."
- "Build a modern state-of-the-art penitentiary in the Northwest, Eastern Shore or Southern Maryland, and transfer all inmates to the modern structure."
- "Establish an in vitro baby-farming system for spouses who cannot have babies and who want them, together with surrogate mothers."

There is much, much more.

Such as giving all handicapped children and adults a state-paid two-week vacation at Maryland resorts and vacation areas.

Such as building a 100,000-seat athletic center in the Baltimore area.

Such as extending the light-rail transit line "to all points of the state."

Such as building a second beltway around Baltimore and another around Washington.

Such as building new monuments to Johns Hopkins and "all Maryland soldiers, sailors, etc., of all wars from the French and Indian Wars to date, either living or dead."

Such as establishing nearly two dozen new museums in Maryland for everything from antique Maryland furniture to a museum on "state wasting assets and minerals" to a museum on scouting. (Mr. Finch is a Silver Palm Eagle scout.)

This is a kitchen-sink platform. Everything remotely possible is thrown in. Aboretums all over the state. Art works in all public buildings. More military cemeteries for veterans. Trade schools and science schools. A low-interest loan fund for the elderly, handicapped and retarded. New helicopters. New highways. New incinerators throughout the state. New hospitals. New libraries. A bigger National Guard.

Expensive, you say? Well, yeah. But Walter Finch gives a five-paragraph answer. Float $18 billion worth of bonds. Pay for it by assessing each man, woman and child an extra $143 for the next 30 years.

Of course, his numbers may be a tad low. The price of building nuclear power plants is steep these days. And a 25,000-bed, high-tech penitentiary would run at least a couple billion or so. Not to mention the billions for all those new roads, bridges, tunnels, — subways, light rails, airports, stadiums, astro-spheres, etc.

Mr. Finch, in his announcement, bills himself as a "veteran lawyer-engineer and decorated hero" of World War II. He also says he is "frequently described as a 'legend' in Maryland state politics."

The Finch legend is sure to grow after this campaign. He may hold the record for biggest-spending gubernatorial candidate of all time.

Walter Finch died on June 2, 1997, at age 79. Ross Pierpont is still at it, running for the U.S. Senate in 1998.

Glendening Looks Past the Primary

July 24, 1994

He's the leader of the pack, the front-runner and likely winner in the September 13 Democratic primary. Parris Glendening has things going his way. His No. 1 primary foe has run an embarrassingly inept campaign that has taken him from first to fourth place in the polls. Mr. Glendening leads his nearest rival by 22 points, and with four candidates in the race his lead looks safe.

And yet, Mr. Glendening still is viewed with suspicion by most voters outside the Washington suburbs. Additionally, the Prince George's county executive may be a household word in College Park and Hyattsville, but when people talk about Parris in Severna Park or Cockeysville they're referring to the city in France, not the gubernatorial candidate.

Political pros panned his selection of a running mate, Kathleen Kennedy Townsend, because it moved Mr. Glendening sharply to the left — at a time when the electorate has been moving steadily to the right. But no one in the Democratic race came up with an all-star running mate, either. What could have turned into a major misstep by Mr. Glendening may have no negative impact in September.

As for Mr. Glendening's $300 million worth of spending commitments to various special interests, it doesn't appear to have turned off primary voters. Marylanders so far are barely cognizant of this election campaign, which works to the county executive's advantage.

The precipitous plunge of Lieutenant Governor Melvin Steinberg's challenge allows Mr. Glendening to start planning for the general election. The other two name candidates in the race, state Senators American Joe Miedusiewski and Mary Boergers, remain regional contenders unable to mount a serious threat.

Mr. Glendening has impressed politicians with his disciplined, well-organized campaign. He is meticulous in keeping lines of communication open to possible allies and delivering thank-you notes and follow-up phone calls to supporters. The primary season has been devoted to cementing, in the public mind, "the vision thing," as George Bush put it. Mr. Glendening has issued a comprehensive issues booklet. It has generated controversy for the spending commitments implicit in Mr. Glendening's vision for Maryland. But he can't make education funding "our top priority" without commiting a bundle of big bucks, and he can't clean up the Chesapeake Bay merely with good intentions.

Mr. Glendening wants to get his conceptual message out: Here is one candidate dedicated to doing what it takes to generate prosperity, to improve the quality of life and make government perform its people-oriented tasks effectively. Thanks to Mr. Steinberg's dwindling challenge, Mr. Glendening can continue emphasizing his themes without "running scared" in the primary.

But what comes after September 13? That's where Mr. Glendening has to shift gears. He will be in fierce combat with the likely Republican winner, U.S. Representative Helen D. Bentley, for the political middle-ground. And at the moment, Ms. Bentley is marginally ahead in the polls.

What will be the Glendening message for the general election? He gave a hint of that last Monday at a political gathering in Brooklandville. The hosts of this affair illustrated Mr. Glendening's growing appeal to traditional Democrats who weren't in his camp a year ago. The party took place at the home of Theodore G. Venetoulis, who was fired last year as Mr. Steinberg's campaign manager. Now he's switched sides. Co-hosts included Jim Smith and Bob and Sandy Hillman — longtime backers of the retiring Governor Schaefer (no friend of Mr. Glendening). The Prince George's executive has extended an open door to Democrats, and they are beginning to flock to his doorway as his lead widens.

More important was the speech delivered by Mr. Glendening that night. He cited his three heroes within the Democratic Party:

Adlai Stevenson, because of the intellect he brought to his two presidential campaigns. Hubert Humphrey, because of the human compassion he imbued in the party. And, surprisingly, Paul Tsongas — because he brought the Democrats back to the political center with his 1992 presidential campaign.

That's precisely what Mr. Glendening will now try to do — move back toward the political center. He was one of the earliest and strongest Tsongas supporters in Maryland. He and his political aides closely analyzed the Tsongas landslide in the 1992 Maryland primary. The lesson is crystal clear: statewide elections from now on will be decided in the suburbs, where voters are trending toward the mildly conservative side of the spectrum.

This means a general election campaign stressing Tsongas-style themes, such as sensibly downsizing government; "reinventing" delivery of government services; confronting budget deficits directly; carefully defining the limits of government. It means specific recommendations in these areas to prove to voters this isn't another political sleight-of-hand.

Helen Bentley would be a tough opponent. Despite her weaknesses, she espouses a conservative message that sounds similar to some of the things Mr. Tsongas was saying in 1992. It will be up to Mr. Glendening to define the core differences in their approaches and prove to voters that he, rather than Ms. Bentley, is the true heir to the Tsongas approach that proved such a big hit in Maryland just two years ago.

The Candidates in the Backstretch...

August 7, 1994

You can't blame Maryland voters for their uncertainty regarding this year's election for governor.

The field is crowded. Some top candidates are unknown to much of the electorate. And little has been written or broadcast about the detailed stances of the candidates.

In fact, one political operative strongly believes the media are part of the problem, not part of the solution.

Michael F. Ford used to be campaign manager for Lieutenant Governor Mickey Steinberg until they had a falling-out over strategy. After his departure last month, Mr. Ford composed a commentary that was never published. Yet his thoughts on the media and this year's election campaign deserve airing:

"Mickey Steinberg isn't much of a campaign manager but he would be a great governor.

"The average Maryland newspaper reader and viewer have no clue about the latter because the issue in the governor's race has become who has the best 'campaign,' not who would be the best governor or who has the best ideas about running this state. Coverage focuses on personalities and the technique of campaigns rather than the substance.

"Many of the newspaper reporters, from whom we expect more, are falling into the tabloidization routine. . . . Political reporters are into process and analysis of process, not ideas or substance other than their own. These are the ones who set the standard for what makes a good or a bad campaign, like handicappers of the *Racing Form*."

Sadly, Mr. Ford is on the mark. The media were transfixed earlier this summer as Mr. Steinberg's campaign imploded. Then focus shifted to who would be picked as running mates. Next came the flap over how many forums Helen Bentley did or did not attend. And now the emphasis is on

American Joe Miedusiewski's hokey humor ads.

What ever happened to real issues? This columnist has been as guilty as others. The focus is on who's ahead, as though it were a horse race. There's a term for this type of coverage — "horse-race journalism."

Professor Doris Graber of the University of Illinois agrees that journalists don't usually waste valuable news space on the details of policy matters raised by candidates. "[T]hese issues are hard to explain and dramatize and rarely produce exciting pictures," she wrote in "Mass Media and American Politics."

"Although these are issues of personal concern to the average voter, most people are unwilling to wrestle with a difficult subject that newspeople have not yet learned to simplify and dramatize. Rather than write complex campaign stories that most of the audience probably would ignore, newspeople prefer to feature the horse-race glamour of campaign developments."

In the current gubernatorial campaign, Mr. Ford says that reporters are hot to track down insider campaign developments but reluctant to plunge into the issues side of things:

"A *Sun* reporter came to my home and woke up my 6-year-old son at 10 p.m. for an interview the night *The Sun* found out I resigned from the Steinberg campaign.

"But when Mickey Steinberg announced his health-care plan that would cut $84 million per annum from the encroaching structural budget deficit, not one newspaper wrote about it. This was in spite of a substantial briefing, copious background material, constant hawking and the media pretense that issues matter."

Other candidates have similar tales to tell.

William S. Shepard can't get reporters to take his campaign statements seriously, though he's had a detailed issues booklet out since early spring. Helen Bentley complains that journalists write about her only when there's something bad to say, not when she's done something of substance that is positive. Ellen Sauerbrey can't figure out how to get reporters to write in depth about the fiscal restructuring of government she preaches.

Polls are what captivate reporters and many readers. These polls, in turn, tell reporters who are the most legitimate candidates. They are the ones who get coverage in a crowded field. The others are largely ignored.

Yet even if *The Sun* were to devote endless inches of news space to policy issues affecting the governance of Maryland, most readers would barely glance at them.

Professor Graber noted, "Overall, three out of four answers people give when asked what they have learned about candidates and issues or why they would vote or refrain from voting for a certain candidate concern personality traits. People are interested in the human qualities of their elected leaders, particularly their trustworthiness, principled character, strength and compassion."

Reporters zero in on these sorts of things. Is Parris Glendening trustworthy? Is Helen Bentley principled? Does Mary Boergers have strength? Does Ellen Sauerbrey have compassion?

The ramifications of the Sauerbrey budget-cutting plan may escape notice; or the specifics of the Glendening economic stimulus proposal; or the Shepard agenda. But by the end of this primary campaign, newspaper readers should have a pretty good idea about the character and overall approach of the major candidates.

It's not an ideal method, but it beats trying to figure out whom to vote for on the basis of infrequent 15-second TV sound-bites.

It still raises the troubling question that Mr. Ford posed: If the media don't pay detailed attention to candidates' stances on issues, how can voters be expected to figure out who is truly best? He admits "it's a problem that both sides" — the media and candidates — "are struggling with."

For Sauerbrey, Now Comes the Hard Part

September 18, 1994

Now that the euphoria has started to subside in the Ellen Sauerbrey camp, it's time to examine some cold, hard facts. Ms. Sauerbrey, regardless of how brilliant her upset primary victory over Helen Bentley may have been, is a decided underdog in the race for governor.

She faces a Democratic opponent who comes out of his own primary in surprisingly good shape, who could outspend her by 3-1, and who has the enormous advantage of a 2-1 edge in the voter-registration rolls.

If anyone should be euphoric, it is Parris Glendening. His well-oiled campaign machine continues to pick up momentum.

Ms. Sauerbrey's triumph in the GOP primary helps the Democratic nominee enormously in solidifying party support: Ms. Bentley posed a much greater threat because of her appeal to Baltimore business leaders, to union leaders and to Reagan Democrats who have voted for her regularly in the past.

A "Democrats for Bentley" committee could well have been led by the state's governor, top Baltimore business executives and virtually the entire political leadership of eastern Baltimore County. That's no longer a worry.

Ms. Sauerbrey's hard-core conservatism is anathema to most regular Democratic pols. The idea of crossing party lines to support her isn't a viable option.

The arithmetic now looks good for Mr. Glendening. He will win a tidal wave of support in his own Prince George's County and in Baltimore. He should win by a healthy margin in Montgomery County, since he would be the first governor from the Washington suburbs in 120 years. Democratic regulars are likely to stick by their candidate in the Baltimore suburbs and in parts of rural Maryland.

Even a pessimistic scenario turns out well for the Democratic nominee. If he holds onto all his primary votes, gets 80 percent of the Mary Boergers

vote, only 40 percent of the Mickey Steinberg vote, just 30 percent of the American Joe Miedusiewski vote and 40 percent of the independent vote, Mr. Glendening still beats Mrs. Sauerbrey — even assuming that she picks up all the Republican votes from her two primary opponents.

But there are some major unknowns that could change the political picture. A Haitian invasion by President Clinton might poison popular opinion against all Democrats in the November election. Mr. Glendening's similarities to Mr. Clinton — they're both "policy wonks," liberals at heart and serious students of government — aren't things he wants to advertise in this campaign.

Even more troubling for the Democrat is the latent anger toward government expressed in the Sauerbrey primary vote and much of the balloting for local offices.

Helen Bentley was viewed as too much a part of the Establishment, too cozy with the unpopular incumbent Democratic governor, too much an insider. She got her head handed to her by Republican voters screaming for drastic change. Will that be reflected by the wider electorate in November?

The Sauerbrey theme in this campaign is clear — cut taxes, slash the bureaucracy, shrink the size of government and get tough on crime. It proved highly appealing in the primary. People want to hear that their taxes will be lower and that bloated government will be put on a starvation diet — even if it's not fiscally possible or prudent.

Ironically, what Ms. Sauerbrey is preaching isn't that far removed from the sermon preached by one of Mr. Glendening's idols, Paul Tsongas. Both are saying: Let's reinvent government that is smaller, less intrusive, less expensive, more efficient, more businesslike.

That seemed to be the direction the Glendening camp was headed when the candidate took the politically risky step two years ago of embracing the Tsongas-for-president movement. He was one of the few top local officials to back Mr. Tsongas, who went on to crush Bill Clinton in the Maryland presidential primary in the fast-growing suburbs, which I labeled at the time as the "Tsongas Belt."

Since then, Mr. Glendening has mysteriously moved his campaign to the left — away from the Tsongas message and toward the liberal spectrum of the Democratic Party. The discontented voters in the Tsongas Belt are up for grabs.

And make no mistake, these voters are still angry at government. If Ms. Sauerbrey delivers her message of lower taxes and smaller government with as much quiet eloquence as she did in the primary, she could ignite the first big conservative trend in statewide politics since the days of U.S. Senator John Marshall Butler in the 1950s. The November 8 balloting will test whether Maryland remains a liberal state or one that is shifting rapidly to the right as discontent among the citizenry grows.

The Pied Piper Toots Her Horn

October 23, 1994

This week's Mason-Dixon poll managed to achieve the impossible: it pleased both gubernatorial candidates.

Republican Ellen Sauerbrey (42 percentage points) sees it as a statistical dead heat with momentum on her side; Democrat Parris Glendening (48 percent) sees it as a steady lead that is fast approaching the magical 50 percent mark that assures victory.

In both cases, there are grounds for serious concern. On balance, though, the Glendening people have more to worry about.

Their traditional Democratic base in the suburbs is eroding in the face of voter discontent and Ms. Sauerbrey's alluring Pied Piper tune of lower taxes. It looks like a strong Republican year across the country and Mr. Glendening could be swept away if the tidal wave washes over Maryland.

Ms. Sauerbrey leads the Democrat in every jurisdiction except three. She leads among white voters, 52-37 percent. She leads among independents, 45-38. She leads among male voters, 46-43 percent. She's preaching an issue that voters like: lower taxes.

The fact that she is so close to Mr. Glendening while being outspent 3-1 in a state that is 2-1 Democratic tells you this is not an ordinary election year. The unexpected could well happen on election day.

Now comes the bad news for Ms. Sauerbrey. Some experts suspect she may have hit her high-water mark, that this is as close as she will get. Mr. Glendening's negative advertising will become incessant in the final two weeks of the campaign. As voters begin to see the holes in the Sauerbrey tax-cut plan, their enthusiasm may turn to skepticism and then opposition. That's the hope, anyway, among the Glendening forces.

Also troubling for Ms. Sauerbrey is the low numbers she gets among women voters (38 percent to her opponent's 53 percent). Women are becoming a deci-

sive factor in elections. They may be the "stealth" factor in this one.

Another deeply disturbing note is Ms. Sauerbrey's abysmal showing among black voters, where she loses by better than 10-1. Even if she wins the election, that lopsided margin could signal bitter racial tensions in Annapolis under a Governor Sauerbrey.

Turnout is the key to this election. Mr. Glendening needs a heavy stream of voters in Baltimore, Prince George's County and Montgomery County. He needs to win by large margins in these three subdivisions, which make up nearly half the state's voting population.

Mason-Dixon gave him 70 percent in the city; 69 percent in Prince George's and 57 percent in Montgomery. But without a big turnout, he won't be able to overcome Ms. Sauerbrey's winning numbers in the rest of Maryland.

Compounding his problem is that there are no local races of consequence in either the city or in Prince George's. Somehow, Mr. Glendening has to excite black voters in these jurisdictions and motivate them sufficiently to turn out in large numbers. His fate could depend on this happening.

Ms. Sauerbrey need not worry about voter turnout. Her supporters will be at the polls, rain or shine. They are highly committed — conservative true-believers; Rush Limbaugh listeners; Christian fundamentalists; NRA members; anti-abortion protesters and voters who are just plain angry at the world. (There are more of them than most polls indicate.)

The secret for the Republican nominee is to keep the public focused on her tax-cut promise. She's out of step with most voters on gun-control and the abortion issue. She's a Neanderthal as far as environmentalists are concerned. But none of that matters if this remains a one-issue campaign.

For Mr. Glendening, it's more complicated. Not only does he have to craft a massive get-out-the-vote strategy, he's got to find a way to win back some of the traditional Democratic voters now leaning in Ms. Sauerbrey's direction. He's failed so far to clearly define his own persona for the public. He seems to be all things to all people. He also has failed to discredit the Sauerbrey tax-cut plan in terms the public can understand.

This election is far from over. It is the most closely contested gubernatorial campaign in this state in 28 years. In 1966, the issue was racial integration in housing ("liberal" Spiro T. Agnew against conservative George P. Mahoney and his theme, "Your home is your castle — protect it!").

This time, the issue is Reaganomics (cut taxes, cut spending and good times will reappear). Will Marylanders dare to take the plunge — despite the failure of Ronald Reagan's economic theories in Washington? Are people so frustrated that they will opt for a radical change without knowing the consequences?

The Pied Piper continues to toot her horn, sending out a mesmerizing message. People want to believe. But is the message too good to be true?

The Big Three Versus Everyone Else

November 6, 1994

Tuesday shapes up as a watershed election for Maryland. Regardless of who wins the race for governor, voting patterns are in the process of shifting so dramatically that this state may never be the same.

Parris Glendening, the Democratic candidate, is relying on a tripod strategy — massive victories in three of the state's most populous jurisdictions that are so huge they offset heavy losses in Maryland's other 21 counties.

If he succeeds, it will establish a new formula for statewide elections and create a Prince George's-Montgomery-Baltimore City nexus in Annapolis.

But if Ellen Sauerbrey, the Republican nominee, wins, the state's rural and exurban counties will command new power. A union of the non-Washington suburbs and the rural counties will come to the fore in Annapolis.

Either way, the next governor will owe election to a different bloc of voters. And, not surprisingly, the next governor will be under enormous pressure to cater to the winning constituencies.

For Mr. Glendening, that means targeting his programs toward the needs of three urban-leaning jurisdictions, two of them with majority-black populations. For Ms. Sauerbrey, it means tailoring programs so that they are pleasing to the conservative Baltimore suburbs and rural Maryland, where voters are overwhelmingly white.

Never before have we seen such a division: the state's three most liberal jurisdictions versus everyone else. The Glendening forces, though, are trying to hold back the Republican tide that is sweeping through much of the nation. If momentum is a factor in this race, give the edge to Ms. Sauerbrey.

And yet it is hard to draw solid conclusions from what's happening. Sure, voters are fed up with the direction of American politics. They are fed up with the inability of Democrats to run the country effectively and efficiently. They are fed up with paying taxes. And an increasing number of voters believe they can get something for nothing — cut taxes and increase conveniences provided by government.

Still, with all this discontent, Maryland voters seem determined to re-elect to the U.S. Senate one of the most liberal politicians in Washington. And a Democrat to boot. Voters are sending mixed signals.

If Ms. Sauerbrey is elected governor it will be because voters are desperate for change. That is precisely what she represents: A radical re-thinking of how government does its job in the State House.

And if the Republican candidate wins, it will be because Democrat Glendening relied too heavily on negative attack ads and never simplified his message in a way that identified him with change.

Instead, he has become the personification of the Democratic hegemony that has ruled Maryland for the past 25 years. Like it or not, he's being punished for the sins of big-spending William Donald Schaefer. Because Mr. Glendening has not established his own persona with voters, he gets labeled as a typical "tax and spend" Democrat.

Even if Mr. Glendening hangs on to win, things will be different in Annapolis. The new gubernatorial order will be Washington-oriented for the first time in this century. It also will be urban-oriented. But it will have little in the way of resources. It will be forced out of necessity to trim government services and revamp bureaucracies to save money. That's one message voters are delivering loud and clear.

For decades, Maryland has been among the most liberal states in the nation. But beneath the surface, the suburbanization of Maryland was slowly transforming the political landscape. The state is a lot more conservative today than it was 20 years ago.

The boom in the suburbs has meant a growing number of married couples, with kids and a house, who no longer want to save the world: they just want to make the mortgage payments and get some money back at tax time. Ellen Sauerbrey appeals to their basic instincts of suburban survival. And she is telling them it can be done without sacrifice.

These people have been increasingly voting for Republican candidates for local offices. It's no accident, for instance, that Arundel, Howard, Harford and Baltimore counties all could have Republican majorities in their councils after Tuesday and that Carroll now is a majority-Republican community.

Thus, it isn't surprising Ellen Sauerbrey has done so well this year. That conservative undercurrent in the Baltimore suburbs is finally bubbling to the surface in a statewide election. Ms. Sauerbrey may be far to the right of most suburbanites on many of her social views, but on the issues that really matter to voters in the 'burbs, she's their kind of candidate. She has given Mr. Glendening the race of his life. Win or lose, she has shaken the old established order to its core.

From Sore Loser to Shadow Governor

November 27, 1994

She's not lurking in the shadows these days, but pretty soon Marylanders may start calling Ellen Sauerbrey the state's shadow governor.

It seems to work well in Britain, so why not in a former colony? When a party — either the Labourites or the Conservatives — loses an election in Britain, the opposition forms a shadow government, complete with a shadow cabinet and a shadow prime minister.

Mrs. Sauerbrey is certainly acting out the role of shadow governor. She grabbed headlines throughout the country last week for attending the Republican governors' conference in Williamsburg just as though she were about to be sworn in.

The fact that she lost the election — even though her most fanatical and ideologically pure followers refuse to admit it and are culling voter lists to prove "fraud" — doesn't faze her at all. In her heart, she knows she won, even if reality dictates otherwise.

And reality does indicate a defeat for Ms. Sauerbrey. Yes, it was close (though not nearly as close as this year's race for governor in Alaska, or a number of other races for Maryland governor earlier in this century). But Mrs. Sauerbrey lost.

It's not very complicated. She got clobbered in urbanized parts of the state and couldn't make up the difference.

Why is it so hard to understand that her lead evaporated around midnight of Election Day when the city votes came in? No conspiracy here — the city's votes always come in later than the rest of the state. The city still uses antediluvian vote-gathering methods and has far, far more precincts than any other jurisdiction — nearly a quarter of the entire state's total.

And why the surprise that Ms. Sauerbrey bombed in many Baltimore neighborhoods? So did George Bush and Ronald Reagan in past elections.

Republicans, who often have been hostile to the city, just aren't popular in these areas.

Still, Ms. Sauerbrey's supporters are zealously weaving a complicated web of conspiracies to explain her non-election. It's all a plot, you see. And like any good conspiracy, there's a Catch-22 that explains how the Evil Empire of Democrats controls all the election levers.

Why, the Democrats appoint the election officials, after all! No wonder Republicans couldn't stop the vote count to accommodate the unreasonable Sauerbrey demands. And the Democrats also appoint all the state judges. Is it any wonder that Republicans couldn't get a fair shake in court on their requests to stop the election results from being certified?

If the Sauerbrey forces had their way, the election results would be dissected vote by vote, even if it took four years of legal wrangling to do it. Of course, that would allow William Donald Schaefer to serve another 48 months — not exactly the ideal solution for all those Schaefer-haters in the Sauerbrey camp.

But barring a stupendous reversal by the courts, Ms. Sauerbrey someday will have to relinquish the front page to Mr. Glendening and take her place as Maryland's shadow governor. She will still attack every Glendening move, aided by an enlarged and more obstructionist Republican minority in the state legislature. But why not adopt the British model?

Ms. Sauerbrey could hold a shadow-governor swearing-in ceremony at the Timonium Fairgrounds Cow Palace and then deliver her inaugural shadow address. A few weeks later, she could give her State of the Shadow State address, perhaps in the St. John's College auditorium three blocks from the state capital. Heck, she might even get Republican legislators to boycott the Glendening address that same day to cheer the shadow governor's speech.

She could name a shadow cabinet: Budget secretary, Thomas Schmidt; licensing secretary, William Fogle; personnel secretary, Roger Hayden; transportation secretary, Helen Bentley; welfare secretary, Alan Keyes; health secretary, Dr. Ross Pierpont; corrections secretary, Robin Ficker; education secretary, Linda Chavez; state police secretary, Paul Rappaport, and economic development secretary, Blair Lee IV.

She could unveil a shadow budget — the one that cuts spending across the board so easily it doesn't even hurt (shadow budget reductions tend to be painless). She could announce, to much applause, her shadow tax cut. And since she doesn't really have to eliminate anything to make it happen, this is one tax cut that is do-able.

The only problem confronting Ms. Sauerbrey is where to establish her official shadow residence. Her farm on Sweet Air Road in rural Baltimore County won't do. No, an Annapolis abode must be found, perhaps even on State Circle. From that perch, Ms. Sauerbrey could keep watch over the Evil Empire until 1998, waiting for her moment of vindication.

The Bad Guys May Be Up to No Good

January 1, 1995

Conspiracy theoreticians are having a field day. Both Republicans and Democrats are getting in on the act.

To hear them tell it, there are dark forces at work in Maryland.

The Republican demonology portrays Democrats as the source of all corruption and malevolence. The Democratic version pictures Republicans as the Dark Side of the political spectrum intent on gaining ascendancy by wrecking the existing power structure.

Let's begin with the Sauerbrey Theory of Election Fraud — more commonly known as the "We Wuz Robbed" school of thought.

Ellen Sauerbrey refuses to admit she lost the gubernatorial election of 1994. She finds it odd that she was ahead until 11:30 election night — before votes poured in from Democratic strongholds. Every glitch in the voting is viewed as part of a vast conspiratorial web.

Even the fact that some polling places in Baltimore didn't open on time because Republican election judges — her own supporters — failed to show up is proof positive that someone was conspiring against her.

Even the fact that a longtime Republican worker and Sauerbrey loyalist took home some documents from the "Election Inquiry Fund" office was deemed grounds to suspect him of being in cahoots with Democrat Parris Glendening.

The police were called in. The Sauerbrey conspiracy theoreticians spread the word that a "spy" had been discovered.

Paranoia is running rampant.

The Sauerbrey lawsuit makes sweeping accusations — with no facts to support her charges. Even her lawyers concede they couldn't find evidence of a Glendening "plot."

And yet her supporters are convinced there was a conspiracy. "Fraud's everywhere," said one dedicated volunteer seeking out Democratic wrongdoing. But if that's true, how was the fraud perpetrated? By whom? No one in the Sauerbrey camp has come forth with proof. She risks being laughed out of court if she can't present a more plausible, documented case. "This is not about politics," Ms. Sauerbrey said at a made-for-TV campaign-style rally to celebrate the filing of her lawsuit. "This is about the power of the people to seat their rightful governor."

Not about politics?

Yeah, and Newt Gingrich and the Republican National Committee are bankrolling her challenge because they want the best candidate to win, regardless of affiliation.

This challenge is all about politics. To the marrow. There's not one aspect of this challenge that isn't wrapped in political strategy and Republican ideology.

At best, the improbable could happen and a judge crowns Ms. Sauerbrey governor. At worst, Parris Glendening is sworn in as governor and the Republicans start a four-year drive to unseat him under the slogan, "We Wuz Robbed."

A defeat in court is in line with the Sauerbrey conspiracy theory. Democrats appointed the state judges, who ruled against her. The judges are registered Democrats. Democrats appointed the local election-board members, who ruled in favor of the Democrat. Democrats defended the state in court against her allegations. And Democrats will do anything to retain power.

And if you lose in court? Then discredit everything Democratic, even the election process itself. Anything to persuade more Marylanders that Parris Glendening symbolizes corrupt politics.

The syllogism runs like this: If all elected officials are crooks, and all top elected officials in Maryland are Democrats, ergo, all corruption in government is caused by Democrats and Governor-elect Glendening.

But there's another conspiracy line in vogue. Let's call it the Glendening Theory of Pure Evil — or the "They're Out to Get Us" hypothesis.

In this construct, the Sauerbrey protests amount to a public-relations ploy. Negative, dirt-throwing campaigning is the new Republican style, a la Newt Gingrich. The objective: Make Mr. Glendening and Democrats look like crooks — even if there is no evidence.

Wage a public-relations campaign that portrays Ms. Sauerbrey as the ever-outgunned underdog and Mr. Glendening as the fat-cat, corrupt pol trying to deny citizens their fundamental rights.

The Democrats expect Sauerbrey forces to drag out the court protest till the eve of the inauguration.

Then they believe Republicans will charge into state and federal courts for an injunction to stop the swearing-in ceremony. The idea is to seize the headlines and media attention, discredit the new governor's integrity and hammer home the point that the underdog was somehow denied justice.

It makes for great photo ops and pro-Sauerbrey news stories that put Mr. Glendening on the defensive, explaining why he isn't a crook.

And if the courts decline to intervene? Next stop: Capitol Hill, where a pliant U.S. Representative Bob Ehrlich of Baltimore County wants to hold hearings on the infamies of the Maryland election. What a Republican circus that would be: A TV extravaganza portraying the defeated Republican as a martyr to the cause.

What a great way to start the "Sauerbrey for '98" gubernatorial campaign! Paranoia, it seems, is running rampant in both political camps.

Ellen Sauerbrey's court suit was dismissed days before the inauguration. She lost to Parris Glendening by 5,993 votes.

Chapter 7

Glendening *in* Office

The Guv and His Generous Pension Plan

February 5, 1995

Parris Glendening has now met the Law of Unintended Consequences — and he will have to live with the ramifications of what happened for a long time.

Who could have predicted the new governor's first crisis would revolve around something that took place years ago in Prince George's County and that has absolutely nothing to do with the governance of Maryland?

Yet the brouhaha over Mr. Glendening's role in pension payouts to aides who followed him from Upper Marlboro to Annapolis isn't a momentary news story. It leaves an indelible impression with a citizenry already cynical about government.

Take Mr. Glendening at his word — that he had nothing to do with these pension developments and inadvertently made three of his aides eligible for these cushy supplemental benefits — and he's still got a massive perception problem.

Take Mr. Glendening at his worst — as a politician neck-deep in concocting this program — and he's got a much larger problem.

Any way you look at it, the governor's image suffers.

Let's go back to the time when this supplemental program began — 1990. Recession had hit Prince George's County. Massive layoffs were under consideration. Concern was voiced about non-merit-system workers who might be laid off. They had no job security and no termination package.

So the Glendening administration and county council created a program to provide a "safety net" for these non-merit-system workers with 15 years of government service. It was modeled after a Montgomery County plan.

It appeared to be the right thing to do — but it wasn't.

Two years later, an unelected county pension board — appointed by Mr. Glendening — dramatically enriched the special benefits. The executive never signed off on these actions; neither did the county council. Giving appointees such unchecked power was fraught with danger.

Then the final, suspicious move: Mr. Glendening, only days before the November election last year, ordered top aides to "resign" — out of courtesy for his successor, he says. But this automatically qualified those with 15 years of county service for the special pension benefits. (Mr. Glendening maintains he wasn't aware of the pension implications.)

For the aides who followed him to Annapolis, it was a charade. They voluntarily left their Prince George's posts — yet because of Mr. Glendening's resignation order, they suddenly qualified for special termination benefits.

On top of that, a friendly ruling by a county lawyer made Mr. Glendening himself eligible for special benefits under the absurd logic that, because of a 1992 term-limitations law, he was forced out of county government and had been "involuntarily separated" — though he had planned for years to leave office and run for governor in 1994. Thus, he can collect $21,000 a year for the next three years. (He says he will decline it.)

Two retired or defeated Prince George's elected officials also qualified for these special benefits since they, too, could claim to have been "involuntarily separated." It's a ridiculous situation.

No elected official — none — should receive such a sweet deal. Every candidate knows that he or she either will be defeated or will some day leave office. It's the chance you take. "Involuntary separation" has nothing to do with it. (Heck, the way they're defining terms in Prince George's, someone fired for stealing government funds would be eligible for benefits, since the culprit was "involuntarily separated" from his job.)

Even more ridiculous is the notion that a pension program had to be created to provide a "safety net" for non-merit-system workers. What was needed was a simple severance plan.

Any worker of long standing deserves a "safety net." Many companies give workers one week severance for each year worked. The idea is to make sure these employees have enough money when they are pushed out the door to serve as a bridge until they find new jobs.

But not a pension that pays someone in his or her 30s or 40s some $20,000 a year for a decade or more. That defies common sense. It reeks of a raid on the taxpayers.

The good news for Mr. Glendening is that all this took place before he became governor. His record in Annapolis is still clean.

The bad news is that this trail of suspicious past deeds has set off alarm bells. Is this part of a longstanding pattern or a regrettable mistake?

While Mr. Glendening personally isn't benefiting any more from this cushy pension program, his three aides are. They already have collected cash for unused sick-leave and vacation days and will receive years of county retirement checks once they quit their state jobs. The amounts are generous by government — or even private-sector — standards.

Efforts last week to limit the damage only partially worked. Whatever the original intent, doling out extra benefits to an exclusive group of government workers sends the wrong signal to state legislators and to Maryland citizens.

Agnew Takes His Place in the State House

February 19, 1995

Who would suspect Parris Glendening of riding to Spiro Agnew's rescue? Mr. Agnew is a charter member of Maryland's Hall of Shame. While governor, he extorted money from state contractors. Why would a good Democrat like Mr. Glendening resurrect a bad Republican like Mr. Agnew?

Because Mr. Glendening's academic training has taught him an important lesson: You can't rewrite history; you can only learn from it.

A couple decades ago, when the ignominy of the Agnew years and the Mandel corruption trials had reached its nadir, Governor Harry R. Hughes dispensed with an embarrassing reminder: He removed the Agnew portrait from the State House reception room. In that lineup of Maryland governors, only Ted Agnew's mug was not to be seen. He became this state's missing link.

But now the new governor's sense of propriety has reversed this exercise in denial. The missing portrait is no longer missing.

In fact, Mr. Agnew wasn't a dreadful governor — except for those white envelopes stuffed with cash. He was one in a long line of moderate and progressive governors this state has had this century.

Maryland has been blessed by a tradition of competence — and centrism — in its elected chief executives. Look at the record in the post-war (World War I, that is) era:

Albert C. Ritchie was a superb governor who initiated a slew of progressive legislation, placed the state on a rigidly conservative fiscal track and dominated politics in the 1920s and early 1930s.

Harry W. Nice, an amiable pro-New Deal Republican, couldn't get along with the General Assembly but it didn't matter: Depression-era stimulus actions from Washington superseded state initiatives.

Herbert R. O'Conor proved a progressive wartime governor with the same fiscal conservatism of the Ritchie era. He achieved reforms in the leg-

islative, executive and judicial branches.

Perhaps the most courageous and far-sighted 20th-century governor was *William Preston Lane*. He dragged Annapolis — kicking and screaming — into the modern era. This Democrat poured money into public schools, implemented a five-year, $200 million road program, created a junior-college system and rebuilt hospitals for the mentally ill and retarded. Given the pent-up needs from the war years, Lane proved the right man for the times. But to pay for this necessary spending, he had to impose a sales tax. That two-percent levy sounded Lane's death knell. He took the political bullet for doing the right thing.

Theodore Roosevelt McKeldin was emblematic of the 1950s, an era of prosperity and growing recognition of tolerance. McKeldin, an eloquent speaker who loved mingling with people, used the governorship as a bully pulpit for civil rights. He also proved a pragmatic Republican governor eager to work with the Democratic legislature on social issues.

J. Millard Tawes, a career state functionary from conservative Crisfield, surprisingly became a reform governor responsible for improving roads and bridges and championing progress in economic development, health and the environment.

Spiro T. Agnew, despite his corruption and blunders on civil-rights matters, improved the workings of government, drew up moderately conservative budgets and claimed partial paternity for the Cooper-Hughes-Agnew-Lee income-tax structure still in effect today.

Marvin Mandel, despite his own corruption woes, championed dramatic changes: The nation's first state school-construction program; 248 independent agencies shoe-horned into 11 cabinet departments; the nation's first state-run auto-insurance fund for high-risk drivers; a less political process for picking judges; subway systems for the Baltimore and Washington areas. Only Mr. Mandel's favoritism for friends and cronies marred his achievements.

Harry R. Hughes, the anti-corruption governor, often left decisions to the General Assembly. He restored respect to the office and kept state finances under control. He was a quiet reformer and typical of Maryland's middle-road governors. Only the enormity of the savings-and-loan crisis late in his term doomed his political career.

William Donald Schaefer. Say what you will about the man, he revamped higher education, built the nationally famed Camden Yards baseball stadium and guided this state through its worst recession since the 1930s without any lingering harm. His personality quirks irked many Marylanders, but the Schaefer years were in sync with nearly all other 20th-century administrations — progressive and moderate in their overall impact.

Mr. Glendening gives every sign of sliding neatly into this list. He appears to be both cautious and progressive. He wants to change government's structure to make it more efficient. That's been a byword of most of the state's better chief executives this century.

Does the Agnew portrait deserve to hang in the same room with Maryland's other governors? Yes, but not just to set the record straight. It's important to keep in mind the progressive path nearly all 20th-century chief executives have followed while in office.

Whether Republican or Democrat, conservative or liberal in their prior political lives, each one of them steered a middle course. That's been the Maryland tradition. It's what this state's voters have opted for time after time at the polls.

Not-Ready-for-Prime-Time Governor

February 26, 1995

That Parris Glendening is one lucky fellow. Those skeletons in his political closet never turned up till after he got sworn in as Maryland's governor. For 12 years, Mr. Glendening presided over populous Prince George's County in the Washington suburbs. And for 12 years, the leading newspaper in that area ignored the internal machinations of the Glendening administration. It would be the equivalent of *The Sun* failing to report on what was really happening in Baltimore County between 1982 and 1994.

What was happening in P.G.?

That's still a question wrapped in ambiguity. We do know that the Glendening administration bought labor tranquility and labor loyalty at an exceedingly high price to taxpayers. We also know that Glendening officials set up a cozy special-benefits package for "involuntarily separated" managers that made the governor and some top aides eligible for enhanced pension payments. And we know that a political culture thrived in P.G. that isn't viewed with approval these days in Annapolis.

Not only did Mr. Glendening manage to emerge relatively unscathed from local newspaper coverage during those 12 years, but his campaign foes in the race for governor last year never dug up any dirt on him, either.

During the 1994 Democratic primary campaign, Mickey Steinberg, Mary Boergers and American Joe Miedusiewski all talked privately about the scandals and embarrassments in Prince George's that they would bring to light. And yet not one episode was ever aired in public by one of the Democrats.

During the general election campaign, Republican Ellen Sauerbrey never dredged up any of this P.G. data, either. Had she spent a fraction of the money she wasted *ex post facto* in challenging Mr. Glendening's election on what had really been occurring in P.G., Ms. Sauerbrey would be sitting by

the fireplace at the Governor's Mansion today.

But she, too, failed to gather the evidence (just as she failed to gather the evidence of election fraud). Once again, the Glendening luck prevailed.

Had any of this information been publicized during the campaign — especially the sweetened pension plan and the no-layoff sweetener contract with labor unions — Parris Glendening would be lecturing students at College Park for a living.

It's too late now. Mr. Glendening is governor for the next four years. But suddenly the honeymoon is over. Public cynicism is returning. Mr. Glendening, it turns out, is more than just a "policy wonk" and expert on public administration. He's a slick pol, too.

How slick? Slick enough to accept a whopping $95,000 from a single contributor and then blithely claim there couldn't possibly be any *quid pro quo* down the road. Slick enough to appoint political hacks to state jobs to help smooth the confirmation of two cabinet secretaries grilled by senators last week on the P.G. pension scam. Slick enough to try to reward his political supporters in his Green Bag appointments, even if it meant naming to the port commission a contractor knee-deep in federal housing allegations of waste and fraud.

Which is the real Parris Glendening? That's a valid question to raise at this early stage of his governorship. Clearly, he's having trouble making the jump from the minor leagues of county government to the big leagues of state government. He's not used to the constant, intense media coverage. He's not used to a rambunctious and often headstrong legislature. He's not used to dealing with presiding legislative officers who jealously guard their prerogatives.

A tight-knit group of lawyers and aides sufficed to run P.G. But not the state. A business-style management structure, with a chief of staff acting as a CEO, can work in P.G., but not in a state capital where no one of rank is going to tolerate such a delegation of electoral authority. Quiet deals with various interest groups kept the lid on P.G. situations, but not in the hot house of Annapolis.

In his first month in office, Mr. Glendening has demonstrated a welcome grasp of the internal workings of government. He has identified some of this state's long untended weaknesses and started to address these deficiencies. But when it comes to matters of politics and public perception, he has repeatedly stumbled.

If the new governor learns from these mistakes, he can put much of the unease behind him. But if he stonewalls and circles the wagons, if he continues to waste political capital on unwise appointments and if he fails to admit his errant ways in Prince George's, these controversies could leave lasting scars.

Up Is Down and Left Is Right

March 26, 1995

Let's try to define some political terms and see how various folks in Annapolis measure up on the important issue of tax cuts.

First, there's *conservative*, which is definitely the thing to be these days. According to my Webster's, it means "conserving or tending to conserve... tending to preserve established traditions or institutions and to resist or oppose any changes in these. . . ."

When it comes to tax cuts, the person closest to that definition is — surprise — Governor Parris Glendening, the guy blasted as a liberal "Spending" in the 1994 election.

He's pushing hardest to conserve state financial reserves, maintain established programs and traditions while vigorously resisting any changes in the way the state runs its fiscal affairs. No tax cuts this year, he says, because he wants to conserve precious tax revenue for fear of what Congress may do.

Next, look at the definition for *liberal* — something you don't want to be accused of any more. Webster says it is someone "favoring reform or progress . . . specif., favoring political reform tending toward democracy, personal freedom of the individual. . . ."

Which group in the State House fits that description?

None other than right-wing Republicans. They want immediate tax relief and deep budget cuts. Why such reform? To return personal freedom to the individual taxpayer. Republican leaders insist taxpayers should decide how to spend the money the governor wants to place in reserve in case of fiscal troubles.

But there's a third term worth pondering — *radical*: Someone "favoring fundamental or extreme change; specif., favoring basic change in the social or economic structure."

You won't find much more basic change in this state's social and economic structure than GOP plans to chop income taxes 24 percent and cut spending to pay for it.

So in this battle, the conservative turns out to be the Democrat derided for leaning too far to the left, and the radical liberals are Republicans on the extreme right.

Further muddying the picture has been the stance of Democratic legislators. House Speaker Casper R. Taylor, a Western Maryland conservative, pushed a plan that could be defined only as liberal. He, too, wanted to turn back tax money to citizens and let them decide how to use it. But he stopped short of the radicalism of the Republicans.

In the state Senate, Barbara Hoffman, a Baltimore liberal and chief budget leader, took a tough stand against the Taylor plan. She sided with the governor in wanting to preserve state revenues. Definitely conservative.

And finally, Senator John A. Cade, the chamber's top fiscal curmudgeon and most powerful Republican, brought some much-needed consistency. Mr. Cade saw the folly in rushing into a tax cut that would be both radical and risky. He opted for a cautious (i.e., conservative) approach: Preserve reserves, keep a tight rein on state spending and wait a year to see what happens in Washington.

In the end, the "conservatives" won. There will be no tax cut this year. Money will be set aside in reserve funds for one of three purposes: In case of recession; in case of federal cutbacks, or in case things go well and the state can afford to lower taxes in 1995. By the time it was over, Speaker Taylor had gravitated to the Glendening side after he was sure his fellow House Democrats understood the dangers of the House Republicans' radical liberalism.

Only the GOP delegates rose to plead for liberal reforms in this state's existing tax and spending policies.

As Alice put it while in Wonderland, "Curiouser and curiouser!"

But if you think there's confusion in Maryland take a peek at the situation in Washington, where Newt Gingrich talks of a "Republican revolution." Revolution by its very nature is a radical notion. And in Mr. Gingrich's context it is a liberal notion, too. He's after extreme changes that lead to more personal freedom from government.

Democrats are left to defend the lonely battlements of the existing order, trying to preserve established institutions. That makes Bill Clinton and friends conservatives.

The Newtonians in Washington have moved so far right they're now on the left; the Clintonians have tried to offset Republican victories by shifting to the right.

Conservatives and liberals. No wonder folks sometimes feel as though they need a scorecard to figure out which side each player is on.

Jack Cade died on Nov. 14, 1996, at age 67.

Making Schaefer Look Small

August 20, 1995

He's the man they love to hate. He is blamed for all that has gone wrong in the past, all that must be fixed up now by the governor and mayor. He's the bad guy; they're the good guys.

Introducing that old devil, William Donald Schaefer.

Both in the State House and at City Hall, there's a concerted effort to denigrate Mr. Schaefer's achievements as governor (two terms) and as Baltimore's mayor (four terms). Baltimore's ills are all the fault of Mr. Schaefer. Maryland's misfortunes are laid at his feet.

Even mentioning his name in state government circles is forbidden. He's been made *persona non grata* in the Glendening administration, even to the point of rejecting Mr. Schaefer's appointment to St. Mary's College board of trustees.

Meanwhile, the Schmoke administration is attempting to re-write history in its own image. Baltimore's woes aren't the fault of a mayor who has been in office nearly eight years — they are the fault of Mr. Schaefer, who failed to solve chronic urban ills when he was running the city.

All this is part of the political jockeying for position by officeholders. By setting up your successor as a failure, you make yourself look good by comparison.

For instance, never let it be said that the reason Governor Parris Glendening had such smooth sailing on his budget this year was that Mr. Schaefer had previously ratcheted down state discretionary spending. Simply by holding the line on spending, Mr. Glendening was able to claim credit for righting the state budget. In fact, the hard work had already been done — by his predecessor.

Take the matter of economic development. Mr. Schaefer had already set an activist tone, yet Mr. Glendening claims to be the one who is energizing

efforts to gain more jobs for Maryland. The very first deal announced by the new governor — keeping McCormick & Co.'s spice distribution plant in Maryland — was largely negotiated by the outgoing Schaefer team after months of discussion and negotiation. Who got the credit? One guess: His name's not Schaefer.

Meanwhile at City Hall, the word being put out is that Mayor Kurt Schmoke is really just trying to undo all the harm done to Baltimore during the 15-year Schaefer administration. The notion that Mr. Schaefer's tenure marked a renaissance for Baltimore is just a "myth," according to the Schmoke propagandists.

This line of thinking is part of strategist Larry S. Gibson's attempt to rally support in the black community around Mr. Schmoke. He's trying to paint a Schaefer-as-devil portrait in which Mr. Schmoke is the hero riding to the rescue of the city's black residents.

The only problem is that it just isn't so. The Schaefer years were, indeed, a time of urban renaissance for Baltimore. But more than that, people remember the Schaefer era as a period when the mayor energized his administration and the bureaucracy and brought city neighborhoods to life. People suddenly sought ways to show their pride in the city and their own communities.

That energy has vanished. The administration and the bureaucracy are slow to react to community concerns — if they react at all. Management of the city continues to deteriorate. Pride for Baltimore and for city neighborhoods is fast receding into the history books.

Try as they might, the Schmoke acolytes can't re-write the past. But it is good politics to attempt to do so in an election year. It helps people forget about Mr. Schmoke's failures in education, crime, drugs, housing and the alarming loss of jobs.

This must be a frustrating time for Donald Schaefer, though. It's no fun to be targeted for demonization by the Schmoke camp. It's downright insulting to have your successor as governor deny you a seat on a small college board. It hurts to know your name can't be spoken in most state offices any more.

And yet this is an enormous tribute. Only by diminishing Mr. Schaefer's stature can his two successors make themselves look larger. Only by ignoring what Mr. Schaefer achieved can they magnify their own modest successes.

Prison Reform That Undermines Itself

February 11, 1996

The problem with Kathleen Kennedy Townsend is that she doesn't remember Gordon Kamka. How could she? She didn't even move to Maryland until three years after Mr. Kamka's controversial reign as prison secretary ended. Yet there is Lieutenant Governor Townsend pushing the same sort of prison "reform" that got Maryland in so much trouble.

For those too young to remember, Governor Harry Hughes hired Mr. Kamka in 1979. Instead of constructing more prisons, Mr. Kamka decided "we can't build our way out of the problem" of overcrowding. Prison-building stopped. Alternative programs were proposed.

That seemed a sensible approach. But it ignored reality. A mushrooming prison population proved relentless. Not enough "alternatives" to prison were put in place. The corrections department under Mr. Kamka was in shambles.

The prison surge was so great that dangerous inmates were shifted to minimum-security camps, thus creating explosive situations. Laxity in work-release programs led to embarrassing scandals. Finally, Governor Hughes sent Mr. Kamka packing, then adopted a get-tough prison policy and went on a catch-up building binge.

Now comes Ms. Townsend, who has shaped a prison vision for Governor Parris Glendening that looks like a return to the Kamka days. It is based on a sound notion, but it flunks the tests of practical politics and penal realities.

Just as Mr. Kamka declared "no new prisons," Ms. Townsend believes there are better alternatives. The problem is that her administration isn't putting any of these "alternatives" in place.

Instead, a 33-member commission (so large it surely will be staff-driven) is supposed to create a plan. But the administration bill dictates the end result: a "truth-in-sentencing" system where the worst offenders get stiff terms but the vast number of offenders get shorter sentences with no parole.

That has led critics to charge that the administration's "tough on criminals" plan actually works to release more inmates faster.

While this commission is deliberating, the governor intends to do nothing about prison overcrowding or about the dearth of alternative programs. That omission could doom the state to years of catch-up construction. When North Carolina went to a truth-in-sentencing system, its prison census soared. Setting up alternatives such as drug-treatment programs, day reporting centers and intensive probation is time-consuming and expensive. The Townsend system has flaws. With no "good-time served" parole, inmates have little reason to remain passive, thus creating even more danger for guards. Judges are deprived of discretion at sentencing time. And the sentencing scheme can lump some people truly deserving of prison with minor offenders.

For instance, a North Carolina judge says that under his state's new program, TV evangelist Jim Bakker — convicted of massive fraud involving hundreds of millions of dollars — would not have spent a day behind bars: He had no prior record. As the judge noted, "He'd be treated the same as a 17-year-old working at McDonald's who embezzles $15."

Still, some criminologists feel that such an approach would rationalize our prison system so that dangerous criminals are locked up for long periods but lesser offenders don't take up expensive space.

The pitfall is that this could make the prison system budget-driven, not public-safety-driven. It is easier to balance the budget if you don't build another $100 million prison. But what do you do if existing prisons are overflowing and you haven't put money into alternatives? You push lesser offenders through the system as fast as you can because there are too few beds and programs for them.

The Townsend-Glendening approach is not getting a good reception. One influential lawmaker said, "The whole thing is a mistake. It's misguided. Stopping prison construction and eliminating boot camp while you let the public believe you're getting tougher on criminals is a fraud."

From a key legislator: "It flies in the face of reality. How can you say you favor alternative sentencing when you close down a forestry camp and cut prison drug programs?"

Budget leaders in the legislature already want the governor to reconsider firing 51 prison teachers, which even the state's corrections chief admits would add to prison overflow because inmates earn "good time" credits through these programs.

The prison population is still growing by 100 a month. A new state law requires longer terms, which exacerbates overcrowding. Demographics point to a surge in the age group most likely to commit crimes. And judges are handing out stiffer sentences. Given these facts, how can you stop planning for new prisons?

Unless the administration comes up with better answers, lawmakers aren't likely to embrace an idealistic "truth-in-sentencing" proposal that seems to make a bad situation worse.

All Things to All People

February 25, 1996

Note to Parris Glendening: It's time to take advice from an American icon about presenting a clear message to constituents. "If you once forfeit the confidence of your fellow citizens, you can never regain their respect and esteem. It is true that you may fool all the people some of the time; you can even fool some of the people all the time; but you can't fool all the people all the time."

A fuzzy message — appearing to try to fool all the people all the time — seems to be part of the governor's problem. He wants to be all things to all people. Like Bill Clinton, he is eager for all groups to like him (and give him campaign support). But sending out conflicting signals ultimately turns counter-productive.

So far this legislative session, the governor has gone in two directions on personnel reform, on environmental regulations, on prison policies and on port dredging. He says he likes to bring opposing sides together under a "big tent" to reach compromise. More often than not, it comes out looking like appeasement.

Take personnel matters. While pursuing reforms to make the state work force more incentive-driven and easier to manage, Mr. Glendening is also pushing a collective-bargaining plan that includes binding arbitration. The two don't mesh. Efficiency gained through reforms would be lost under a raft of inflexible work rules bargained away — or awarded by an arbitrator. Any savings from reforms vanish into almost certain wage and benefit hikes each year.

On prison policy, the governor preaches a get-tough approach. But his "truth in sentencing" bill actually would mean shorter and less restrictive sentences for most lawbreakers. He calls for harsher treatment of hardened criminals, but he has stripped nearly all money from his budget for prison construction. And while his lieutenant governor crusades for alternatives to incarceration, there's no money for new alternative programs in the administration's budget.

The same duality crops up in regulatory reform. The governor wants to please the business community, but also the environmentalists. Thus, he has gone halfway on lifting regulations that impede businesses. So business leaders grumble that the governor's moves don't go far enough, and environmentalists complain that he is giving away too much.

The same straddle can be seen on harbor-dredging. Maryland needs a long-term solution for disposing of material dredged from the bay's shipping channels. Delays could damage the state's maritime economy. And yet the governor rejected a carefully crafted compromise worked out over several years by state officials, bay scientists and port leaders because environmentalists objected to experimental dumping of spoils in the deepest part of the bay. That move cheered environmentalists but dismayed the port community. The apparent waffling could produce continued gridlock on the critical dredging question.

The same thing could happen on prisons and personnel reform. The governor has fuzzed his message and given lawmakers the impression he has no clear vision.

But, as Abraham Lincoln said over a century ago, you can't fool all the people all the time. Mr. Glendening comes off as weak and hypocritical. Lawmakers see through the charade. They have little confidence in this administration. Because there is no statement of the governor's real priorities, legislators assume his agenda is merely political — to assuage as many groups as possible.

Given that unfocused direction, lawmakers have little incentive to reconcile the governor's divergent approaches, or to side with one group over another. That is tough, thankless work. Unless the governor takes strong stands, why should legislators?

Mr. Glendening is not popular with the public. A recent poll showed his favorable rating at just 32 percent. His efforts to build two new football stadiums, while of long-term importance, aren't yet viewed positively by most voters.

To regain public confidence, he needs to chart a firm course with clear goals and objectives that Marylanders applaud. So far, that hasn't happened. Mr. Glendening has muddied his message. He has, indeed, tried too often to be all things to all people.

They Made Annapolis Work

May 5, 1996

Janet and Ratch are retiring — and political Annapolis will never be the same. When it comes to crunching numbers and explaining what they mean, these two have no peers.

Janet L. Hoffman established herself as the Einstein of government lobbyists, the fiscal wizard for Baltimore, whose political and financial savvy was the envy of the State House. Her influence was immense. Governors plotted strategy with her help, legislators far removed from Baltimore turned to her for guidance.

William S. Ratchford II held sway as the legislature's Information Man, the repository of all knowledge on complex fiscal formulas and the analyst best positioned to offer guidance on tax and spending bills.

Together, they have been around the State House 81 years. Institutional memory? They cornered the market.

On paper, the two were support staffers. In fact, they were crucial players in the annual General Assembly merry-go-round. Ms. Hoffman wasn't simply the city's lobbyist, she was a powerful presence. They didn't call her the "48th Senator" for nothing.

Mr. Ratchford didn't simply recite reams of statistics to legislators. He carefully analyzed fiscal programs and then in unusually clear language explained the impact and implications to lawmakers in ways they could understand. No major money or budget bill moved through the Assembly without his input.

This past General Assembly session was Janet Hoffman's last, after 47 years. When she began as the entire support staff for the new Fiscal Research Bureau in 1949, Parris Glendening was starting grade school, William Donald Schaefer was a struggling title-search lawyer and Kurt Schmoke hadn't been born yet. Louie Goldstein was a first-term senator from rural Calvert County.

By the time Bill Ratchford arrived on the Annapolis scene in 1962, Ms. Hoffman had just gone to work as Baltimore's one-person lobbying team (it is now 10 times that size). He was lobbying for the State Association of County Commissioners of Maryland, which had the unfortunate acronym of SACCOM — as in "sack'em." Now it is called the Maryland Association of Counties, or MACO.

Six years later, he joined the new Department of Fiscal Services as director of fiscal research — the old Fiscal Research Bureau. He had a staff of 12. Now he's got 120 analysts to comb through bills and budgets for lawmakers and an overall staff of 224.

Both are Annapolis legends. Foremost, they are trusted, respected for integrity and dedication to the legislature. They can recall the detailed history behind a law, describe how it works, dispassionately note unforeseen ramifications of proposed changes and suggest ways to circumvent these problems.

Government lobbyists in Annapolis "went to school" on Janet Hoffman. They watched her maneuvering and her three-dimensional chess moves. They saw how year after year she won big benefits for Baltimore, even as the city's delegation shrank.

Similarly, Bill Ratchford served as the model for countless analysts who learned by working their way through his department. State budget secretary Fred Puddester is one alumnus. Many of the top fiscal aides for the governor and the county executives came out of the Ratchford School of Budget Research.

Ms. Hoffman finished her long lobbying career in April, but Mr. Ratchford may yet return for his 36th session. He is taking advantage of the just-passed early-retirement bill, but a provision in it would allow legislative leaders to keep him in his job through the 1997 General Assembly.

Replacing them will be impossible, because there's no way to find two other individuals with that kind of legislative memory. Their skills will also be missed. In fact, the city's efforts have faltered since Ms. Hoffman stepped down as chief lobbyist a decade ago.

Solid staff work is the backbone of any successful legislature. Maryland's has long been noted for its top-notch support staff. And Baltimore has a deserved reputation for its string of successes attributable to its first-rate staff. Janet Hoffman and Bill Ratchford made it happen. Stepping into the shoes of legends won't be easy.

Don't Kiss Preakness Goodbye

May 26, 1996

Joe De Francis had a great Preakness. The weather turned sunny. The crowd topped 80,000. Betting — thanks to simulcast wagering elsewhere in Maryland and throughout the country — was huge. And it was a wonderful race, with an exciting wire-to-wire victory by Louis Quatorze.

And yet, all is not well at Old Hilltop. A random peek at a recent day at the races shows the extent of the track's decline. Only 3,100 fans showed up, betting a measly $224,000. Those are anemic numbers. In fact, except for Saturday races and the Preakness, Pimlico is a losing proposition for Mr. De Francis.

The steep descent of Pimlico underlines racing's poor demographics. Its fans are dominated by older men in retirement. Racing doesn't draw the young. There's not enough going on at the track to attract them. Too many other leisure-time activities compete for their attention.

Compounding Mr. De Francis' woes are the slot machines raking in millions at Delaware Park. A big chunk of that money will end up in the race track's purses later this summer and next year. Before long, Delaware Park's purses could be double Pimlico's. That will lure the best Maryland trainers and jockeys — and bettors.

Pimlico could turn into a third-rate track, a rundown facility that doesn't do enough business to justify a huge capital infusion.

No wonder a worried Mr. De Francis is mentioning the possibility of eventually closing Pimlico, and transferring all his racing dates — including the Preakness — to Laurel. Rather than endure a lingering, painful death, Pimlico might be better off with a quick and clean demise.

Free-market purists say a dying industry like racing should be allowed to succumb. Why try to save it through government intervention?

That's persuasive in the abstract. But when you add up all the jobs linked

to a healthy Pimlico — the stable crew, vendors, clerks, track staff — plus the farm jobs linked to the racing industry and the thousands of acres of farmland dedicated to raising horses, killing Pimlico isn't so clear-cut. Kiss Pimlico goodbye and you could lose much of that green farmland. And how are we going to make up all the jobs lost?

So far, the political response to Pimlico's decline has been discouraging. When Mayor Kurt Schmoke was approached about some sort of city assistance to Pimlico, his initial response was to urge that the Preakness not be moved from Baltimore until after the city's bicentennial celebration next year. Period.

As for state assistance, there's no enthusiasm from the governor or legislature for massive aid to rebuild Pimlico and pump millions into race purses each year.

That leaves one option — slots at the tracks. If business is booming in tiny Delaware, imagine the slots action at Pimlico, Laurel and Rosecroft. Early estimates are that slots would generate a big enough revenue stream to finance a $100 million re-construction of Pimlico, boost purses to New York-style levels and give the city and state big chunks of change.

There's a good argument to be made for slots at the tracks. These facilities are isolated enclaves where gambling already takes place. It is well organized gambling that is well policed. If slots were tied to the state lottery's computers, the chances of criminal activity (such as skimming of proceeds) would be minimized.

The problem is that confining slot machines to race tracks in Maryland is proving difficult. Greed is taking hold.

The mayor wants an inner harbor-area slots palace. The House speaker wants one in Western Maryland. Powerful lobbyists want them in Cambridge and along the Potomac River. Firefighters want slots in fire halls. Veterans groups want them in their halls, too, throughout the state. And what about all those neighborhood taverns with their own video poker machines and illegal payoffs? Bar owners will insist on having legal slots, too.

Once the door is open, there's no end in sight. Such an explosion of new gambling won't be tolerated by voters. A governor or legislature that adopts such a plan risks defeat at the next election. A slots-legalization bill would surely be petitioned to referendum and be clobbered by voters — who might then take out their fury on slots supporters on the ballot.

All this puts Mr. De Francis in an uncomfortable — and possibly untenable — position. The Preakness may be nearing the end of its ride at Pimlico. The tragedy is that so few public leaders seem to care.

Unlucky Legacies of a Lucky Man

September 22, 1996

"My kind of man, Ted Agnew is . . . my kind of man." Those were the days . . . when Spiro T. Agnew was considered the lone hope of the liberal establishment in Maryland . . . when Ted Agnew was regarded as an effective and moderate Baltimore county executive who valiantly stood up for right and justice against the dark, racist sloganeering of the Democratic Party's nominee for governor, George P. Mahoney.

That Agnew won the governor's race in 1966 was a political fluke, as had been his election as county executive in 1962. He had the good fortune to run for office at a time when local Democrats were bitterly split. He and Richard Nixon also had the good fortune to run for president and vice president in 1968 at a time when national Democrats were bitterly splintered over the war in Vietnam.

Ted Agnew was a lucky man. His luck ran out when federal prosecutors inadvertently uncovered a bribery and kickback scheme run for Agnew while he was county executive (and later governor). That infamy followed him to his grave last week.

There were two sides to Ted Agnew.

The good Ted pushed through a civil-rights bill in a conservative and narrow-minded suburban county. The son of Greek immigrant Theofrastos Anagnostopopoulos was praised for his far-sighted work on the county zoning board. The new governor helped to implement a progressive income tax (the Cooper-Hughes-Agnew-Lee) bill.

Then there was the bad Ted, denouncing protests at segregated Gwynn Oak Amusement Park, and rebuking his own human-rights commission for siding with the protesters. There was his harsh criticism of black leaders for "allowing" the Baltimore riots of 1968. And there was the mean-spirited, negative campaign he conducted as Richard Nixon's hatchet man. He was the precursor to Rush Limbaugh, the first conservative in such high office to cruelly attack those who disagreed.

Hubert Humphrey was "squishy-soft on communism"; anti-war protesters were "the delegation from Hanoi." He said, "When you've seen one city slum, you've seen them all." He joked about liberal "fags," ridiculed prominent Democrats and essentially told off anyone he saw as a threat to white middle-class America.

There is a nastiness, indeed a viciousness, in some of today's conservative Republican politics that traces its lineage through Ted Agnew. When elevated to the national scene, he found an audience that loved to hear him excoriate his foes, painting them as evil threats to America's security. The superheated, destructive rhetoric of zealous conservatives, sadly, is one of Agnew's legacies.

His larger legacy is of corruption in high office. He shattered many Americans' illusions about the purity of our very top elected leaders. Public cynicism toward politicians flows from Agnew's criminality.

To the end, Ted Agnew deeply resented any implication he was a crook or had been found "guilty" in a court of law — even though the sentencing judge said Agnew's *nolo contendere* plea was tantamount to an admission of guilt. A year ago, Agnew wrote to me after reading a column of mine defending the decision by Governor Parris Glendening to finally hang Agnew's portrait in the State House reception room. Here are excerpts:

"What disturbs me is that the facts have become distorted over [22] years due to repetitions of errors in reporting. For example, I never extorted money from contractors and have never been convicted of that crime or of bribery. I was convicted of a single count of tax evasion...

"With regard to your reference to my 'blunders on civil-rights matters,' I would remind you that I fought very hard for public accommodations during the Gwynn Oak Park disturbances, and for open housing, even though such stands were highly unpopular in Baltimore County...

"Also, I have a hard time understanding the selective outrage that resulted from my seeking political contributions from those doing business with the state government. That the money did not go into my pocket was evident from the fact that I left office broke and had to borrow [from Frank Sinatra] to re-establish myself.

"Certainly, it was wrong, but where was the clamor about [former Governors] McKeldin and Tawes. Everyone on your paper was fully aware [that they] . . . sold every political appointment... The same procedures were in place under [Agnew's predecessors] in Baltimore County. I never sold an appointment or a job...

"Sometimes I wonder whether it ever occurs to editorialists and cartoonists that the hurt they inflict over a long period of time extends to the target's family.

"I have been married for [54] years to a wonderful woman, who has suffered immensely and silently because she happens to be Spiro Agnew's wife. The hurt has also touched my children and grand-children. Isn't it time to ease up on the vicious barbs and cartooning?..."

For Ted Agnew, the battle to defend his honor is over. The barbs have finally ceased. In time, history will render its judgment.

Spiro Agnew died on September 17, 1996, at age 77.

A Better Governor Than He Seems

September 29, 1996

No one in Maryland was happier to see the official start of fall than Gov. Parris N. Glendening. His was a dreadful summer, filled with embarrassing stories, controversies and missteps. More than a few powerful Democrats worry that the governor now has sunk so low in public esteem that a Republican romp is likely in 1998.

What has Parris done wrong? Why do so many people say such mean things about him?

Most of the complaints concern integrity. Is he applying too much pressure by personally squeezing big campaign donations from business leaders who deal with the state? Did he let his aides in Prince George's County receive excessive cash payouts when they left government? Does he go too far in catering to special interests who helped get him elected? Does he try too hard to please every supplicant, making promises he knows he can't keep?

These are troubling questions. Public debate during the warm months focused exclusively on them. Left unexamined has been Mr. Glendening's work in office.

Maybe it's not sexy or exciting enough to catch the attention of citizens. But Mr. Glendening has compiled a pretty good record.

And he has been straight as an arrow on his campaign promises. In the glossy, 50-page campaign booklet he put out in 1994, "A Vision for Maryland's Future," Mr. Glendening committed to a "Five E" plan — education, enforcement, economic development, environment and excellence in government. He hasn't strayed far from these points.

In education, he vowed to expand community, business and college involvement in schools; remove disruptive students; emphasize career and technical education; increase state education aid, and "revamp school construction planning to keep older neighborhood schools strong."

In higher education, he said he'd minimize budget fluctuations in college allotments, provide strong support for community colleges and seek to reform the legislative scholarship program.

Without exception, the governor has followed through.

Similarly, he pledged to revamp the state's business agency, devise a strategic business plan, enhance the Port of Baltimore's competitiveness, offer job-creating incentives and tax rebates to companies, and make state taxes more business-friendly.

Again, he's right on target, right where he told voters he'd be.

Look at law enforcement. He said he would allow only one handgun purchase per month, ban all assault weapons and try to ban certain types of "killer" ammunition — and he did. He pledged to push for truth-in-sentencing legislation — and he did.

Even in the environmental field, where he's been sharply criticized, the governor laid out a clear plan. He said he'd simplify regulatory enforcement of environmental laws. He said he was committed to making older neighborhoods more attractive to live and work in. He said he would try to direct future development to areas with infrastructure already in place. He followed his own blueprint.

Here's more: He said he'd reform the welfare system, invest in updated technology, reform the state personnel system and "gradually streamline the state work force." Mr. Glendening did as he had promised.

That's pretty good for a politician. It may not be exciting or sensational, but Mr. Glendening can't be faulted for not delivering on his campaign themes.

Perhaps we expect too much from our elected leaders. Perhaps in our cynicism we go overboard in finding fault with office holders. Perhaps in Mr. Glendening's case he was too much of an unknown to most citizens. Or perhaps we have become so fascinated with "integrity" issues that we ignore the dull, substantive decisions that make a difference in people's lives.

Parris Glendening said two years ago that he wasn't an exciting candidate but he was the best organized. He knew what he wanted to do. He even set out his objectives in 50 pages — and since then has gone about implementing them, one by one, step by step.

We haven't been paying much attention to this effort. And his big campaign fund-raiser tomorrow night will once again divert the spotlight away from the governor's record and onto his list of political contributors.

But Bill Clinton is in the midst of proving that performance in office can overcome questions of integrity. Could a similar strategy work for Parris Glendening in 1998?

Guv Girds for the Monster of Many Heads

January 5, 1997

Parris Glendening could be in for a pummeling. He's not beloved by state legislators, who begin their 90-day session Wednesday. He's proposing far-reaching and very costly programs. And, most important, Maryland's General Assembly has gotten used to chewing up governors.

Not since Marvin Mandel in the 1970s has a governor dictated what the legislature would approve or disapprove. From that point on, there has been a steady decline in gubernatorial influence and a steady rise in the power of the General Assembly.

Much of this shift has to do with the backgrounds and personalities of Mr. Mandel's successors: Harry Hughes, William Donald Schaefer and Mr. Glendening. Two of them lacked any Annapolis experience. None of them used the kind of arm-twisting and horse-trading that made Mr. Mandel (who had been a masterful Speaker of the House) so successful. And none of them tried to reclaim power from the legislature.

Mr. Hughes, a passive man who had once served as Senate majority leader, believed in submitting his bills and then letting the General Assembly alone. "The governor," he told historian George H. Callcott, "is not the policy-making body in the state; policy is for the General Assembly to establish."

Into that vacuum stepped House Speaker Ben Cardin, who quietly set state policy in those years. The executive's authority had been seriously eroded.

Mr. Schaefer tried to recover that power, but failed. He never fully grasped the delicate dynamics of the General Assembly. His weak staff, dominated by aides he brought with him from Baltimore, never learned how to finesse the state legislature. (The one person who did know how, Lieutenant Governor Mickey Steinberg, was ignored after the first year.) And Mr. Schaefer's eccentricities either irritated or infuriated lawmakers.

Mr. Glendening, too, lacks a staff with the kind of jugular instinct that served Mr. Mandel so well. And like Mr. Schaefer, Mr. Glendening doesn't fully appreciate the ebbs and flows of the legislative session and the political needs of individual legislators.

He has further alienated lawmakers by leaving them in the dark on major initiatives. That is a big mistake with a legislature used to playing a dominant role in fashioning government policy.

Today's lawmakers want to share the spotlight. It feeds their egos, elevates their status in Annapolis and helps them raise campaign funds and impress voters.

But Mr. Glendening likes to get full credit in the media. He's famous for snubbing legislative leaders at important ceremonies and ignoring key members before announcing proposals.

Lawmakers have moved aggressively to control the state budget. They often try to micromanage agencies, though that is supposed to be the exclusive province of the executive. No governor has mounted a legal challenge to this legislative intrusion. Thus, the breadth of the General Assembly's power continues to widen — at the governor's expense.

That could make it difficult for Mr. Glendening to get his way this session. His view of the state budget could be on a collision course with Assembly budget panels. And that means a major clash over cuts in agency spending and plans to reduce the state income tax, start a free-tuition program for B-average college students and other high-cost initiatives.

Through the years, legislators have beefed up their support services. In fact, the Assembly's budget forecasters now tend to be more accurate than the governor's. That further emboldens lawmakers to rewrite the administration's budget so it fits their revenue and spending estimates.

A tug of war between the two branches of government is an essential aspect of the checks and balances written into the state constitution. But ever since reapportionment in the 1960s, the legislature has been evolving into a far more assertive entity.

No longer is the governor the all-powerful chief executive. Today, he is forced to share power with legislative leaders.

So don't be surprised if Mr. Glendening's tax-cut plan is politely ignored. And don't be shocked if some of his other proposals are rewritten or set aside for further study.

Even a Marvin Mandel might have trouble bringing today's General Assembly to heel. And Parris Glendening has shown that in dealing with the legislature, he is no Marvin Mandel.

Chapter 8

Scoundrels, Statesmen and Controversies

The Man Who Handles Maryland's Money

July 13, 1997

Remember this name: Richard N. Dixon. You could be hearing a lot from him in the months and years ahead. Mr. Dixon is the state treasurer, a potentially powerful post that most citizens don't even know exists. The position is filled every four years by the General Assembly — from whence Mr. Dixon came — not by voters. Thus, the anonymity.

But with the $100,000-a-year job comes membership on some potent bodies, including the state's Board of Public Works and the state's pension board. The treasurer also reinvests Maryland's revenue — about $250 million comes in every day — in super-safe but high-yielding government securities.

The new treasurer is shaking things up. He is micro-managing the state's daily investments, which comes naturally to someone who spent 26 years as a stock broker. He's installing a modern reconciliation system — something that should have been done years ago in an office that handles nearly $60 billion a year.

Mr. Dixon is the first treasurer in 24 years to have a finance background. Before then, part-time bankers had held the post, depositing gobs of state money in non-interest-bearing accounts at their own and other local banks. An expose by reporter Doug Watson changed all that.

Treasurer Dixon also is a force on the pension boards and the powerful three-member Board of Public Works, as became clear last week, when he publicly took on Governor Parris Glendening and Comptroller Louis L. Goldstein. He accused the governor of having "wimped out" by not backing his attempt to block the renomination of a pension-board member he accused of trying to prevent black-owned investment firms from gaining a piece of the state's $24 billion retirement-account business.

Mr. Dixon thinks the pension board tends to favor New York and other out-of-state investment firms over local financial companies. Few of the board members have professional investment backgrounds. Nor do they feel an obligation to promote local investment companies. That makes Mr. Dixon bridle. He also can't understand why the pension board kept so much of its money out of the current bull market, the longest in history. Only now is the board slowly shifting some $1 billion from bonds to stocks.

And he is vigorously opposed to a plan to liberalize state pension benefits by raising state payments substantially. His concern: This could alarm bond-rating houses and threaten Maryland's triple-A bond rating by greatly enlarging the state's unfunded pension liabilities.

Mr. Dixon, 59, is no liberal. He is fiscally conservative, both as investor and as politician. He easily won four terms to the House of Delegates from conservative Carroll County and was one of very few Democrats to win office there in recent years. In 1994, he racked up 7,000 more votes in his legislative district than Mr. Glendening received in the entire county.

He also is one of a handful of blacks to gain election in heavily white-majority districts. Carroll County is 97 percent white. It helped that his family has lived there for generations, that he is a member of the National Rifle Association, that he had the 14th most conservative voting record in the legislature, that he refused to join the Legislative Black Caucus because its liberal agenda contradicts his own and that he became an influential budget subcommittee chairman.

In some ways, he is this state's Clarence Thomas — a black conservative unafraid to express his political views. Unlike Justice Thomas, Mr. Dixon has learned how to work effectively within the system. This past week's outburst was atypical. Usually, he keeps his disagreements out of public view. Such an approach often proves more effective than the Lone Ranger style of Justice Thomas.

As the ubiquitous Louis L. Goldstein starts to slow down a bit (everyone does at 84), Mr. Dixon's profile may rise as a vocal defender of conservative, but sensible, state fiscal policies — in money management, in pension-board actions and in decisions of the Board of Public Works. As we discovered this past week, when provoked, he is no shrinking violet.

Where Are the Champions for UM?

August 31, 1997

Maryland is missing the boat when it comes to public higher education. This has been going on for decades.

Even when University of Maryland President H.C. "Curley" Byrd was a political power in the 1930s, 1940s and 1950s, the university's pride wasn't academic prowess — aside from a prodigious building program — but a national football championship.

Much has changed since then, thanks to the scholarly bent of Byrd's successors, Wilson H. Elkins and John S. Toll. Classroom quality has risen dramatically.

Yet these improvements came with only grudging support from state government. No one since Curley Byrd has had the clout to deliver the funds necessary to turn UM into a pre-eminent public university system. Governor after governor has eagerly put money into new buildings, but not into the operating funds that might make UM second to none.

Legislators in America hesitate to pour new tax dollars into university enhancements. The return on investment isn't easy to see. Neither are the political rewards.

That's why state education funds for K-12 increased $168 million this year, but higher education received only $23 million more. There are far more votes linked to local schools, with 800,000 students, than to a university system with 80,000 students.

University leaders reluctantly accept this reality. Instead of lobbying for massive new aid, they settle for the crumbs.

Case in point. William E. "Brit" Kirwan, president of UM's flagship College Park campus, railed in a recent letter to the editor about a passing reference in my column last week to a "big pay raise" planned for state workers. He took offense at my calling that wage hike — which will go to

College Park employees, too — "big." Well, the dollar increase next year will amount to nearly $100 million — that's big. But Dr. Kirwan is looking at the percentage increase — roughly 2 percent — not so big.

But this misses the broader picture. A cost-of-living increase doesn't move College Park into the top ranks of public universities. To do that would take a far greater state commitment. Yet there is no campaign at College Park to make it happen.

Chancellor Donald N. Langenberg, who runs the 11-campus system, and Lance Billingsley, who chairs the system's board of regents, are loath to criticize the governor for failing to provide UM with the money needed to become truly first-rate. They say they "understand" the financial binds that dictate very modest new investments. And so public colleges have raised tuition substantially in recent years.

When the latest round of hikes was announced, Annapolis pols were quick to criticize. Yet who's to blame for these tuition increases, if not those same politicians?

Higher tuition charges flow directly from the lack of new state college aid. Since 1990, state aid as a percentage of total higher-education support dropped by 27 percent; to compensate, public colleges were forced to raise tuition 23 percent.

To his credit, William Donald Schaefer tried in the late 1980s as governor to boost higher education funding. But after two years of bountiful budget increases, the recession forced him to give up. Over the next two years, higher-education aid decreased $105 million. No effort has been made since then to dramatically enhance quality at the University of Maryland. Annapolis never gave UM a promised $141 million to elevate its academic stature.

Spirits soared when Parris Glendening, who taught at College Park, became governor. But a weak economy meant that he could pledge to give UM only modest, steady raises to offset inflation. That comes to $21 million this budget year. Not much when split among 11 campuses.

The regents aren't asking for much more next year, either — a mere $26 million. It won't turn a good university into a great one.

This short-sighted approach by everyone involved keeps Maryland at a disadvantage in its economic-development efforts.

For instance, Ciena Corp. of Linthicum — one of the hottest start-up companies around — announced that it won't open a technology-development center in Maryland because of the lack of qualified engineers coming out of local colleges. Those high-paying jobs are going to Atlanta.

Other companies report similar stories. Yet where is the hue and cry from the business community to put university funding at the top of Maryland's priority list? Instead, business' top concern has been cutting the state income-tax rate — a move that, ironically, will make it harder for Annapolis to boost higher-education aid.

No one, it seems, is championing University of Maryland. Sure, Senate President Thomas V. Mike Miller is hot to ante up state money for a new fieldhouse for his alma mater. But where are the prominent corporate or political figures lobbying for a vast new spending plan to make University of Maryland the envy of its academic peers? Don't they see the value in such an effort?

Or is the political price of crusading for more state higher-education aid too high?

Brit Kirwan left College Park for the presidency of Ohio State University in the spring of 1998.

'Montgomery Tilt' won't fly in Maryland

November 16, 1997

Doug Duncan has a vision. It could be called the "Our Fair Share" campaign. Or the "Greater Washington Political Alliance." Or simply "Beat Baltimore."

Behind this vision lies his desire for a fundamental shift in Maryland politics — away from a "Baltimore Tilt" toward a decidedly "Montgomery Tilt."

Mr. Duncan wants to fashion a new coalition (sort of a Maryland version of Greater Serbia) that would propel Montgomery County into the catbird seat.

That should not come as a surprise, since the creator of this vision happens to be Montgomery's county executive.

It makes for excellent politics in preparation for next year's election campaign. Mr. Duncan can use his crusade to good advantage in Montgomery precincts where the "more from Annapolis" mantra and the "beat up on Baltimore" rhetoric stir passions.

Beyond the county's boundaries, though, Mr. Duncan's message may not resonate nearly as well. The view from Montgomery often is at odds with the view from everywhere else in the state.

Indeed, there may be more differences than similarities in the jurisdictions Mr. Duncan seeks to meld together.

These counties are dominated by Republicans and conservative Democrats, who look with extreme skepticism at a coalition run by liberal Montgomery.

Then there is the wealth factor. Montgomery is very rich. The affluent of the Washington suburbs flock there.

There is also Montgomery's greater sophistication and Washington orientation versus the more rural, Annapolis orientation of counties Mr. Duncan is wooing.

And, finally, Mr. Duncan runs smack into a General Assembly mindset that favors statewide approaches rather than divisive regional power plays.

He faces an uphill battle.

Mr. Duncan's approach may sound good in theory, but what happens when he proposes a school-aid formula that rewards Montgomery and Prince George's far more than other coalition partners? Or a shift in the road-building allocation that stresses Montgomery's highway needs?

Maryland's long history is inextricably tied to Baltimore City. It remains by far the state's largest city, its only densely populated urban center. It also remains the economic, cultural, social and political focal point for the expanding metropolitan region.

"Going downtown" to folks in Aberdeen, Westminster or Severn means Baltimore, not Montgomery. When Marylanders talk about "the port," it's the Port of Baltimore. "The Stadium" means Camden Yards. "The airport" is Baltimore-Washington International.

Maryland continues to be Baltimore-centric. Turning the state into a Montgomery-centric entity is a stretch.

There is no urban center of half-a-million people in Montgomery, no Harborplace where people congregate on weekends, no sports venue to lure people, no tourist draws, no Walters Art Gallery or Mechanic Theater, no tightly packed downtown office towers, no universities, no core.

What Montgomery does have is a wide collection of upscale neighborhoods; a number of middle-income, aging neighborhoods; outstanding public schools; a great suburban environment; booming high-tech business development, and enormous needs created by all this rapid growth and high quality of life.

But it is not, and will never be, the heart and soul of this state.

The trouble with Mr. Duncan's coalition-building is that he is talking to the wrong people the wrong way.

His county is far more a mirror-image of Baltimore County than St. Mary's County. Coalition-partner Prince George's has more in common with city politicians than with Montgomery pols. Calvert County's natural ally is Anne Arundel, not Montgomery.

That points to the need for a super-regional coalition which resolves problems through consensus-building, not by creating the impression this is an "us-against-them" struggle in which Baltimore is portrayed as the enemy.

Mr. Duncan gave up too quickly on a super-regional alliance last legislative session in a dispute over school aid. Bringing jurisdictions in the Greater Baltimore and Greater Washington orbits together is far preferable to his recent, more modest efforts that strike some as divisive.

Identifying solutions to suburban-urban problems shared by the Big Seven subdivisions and the fast-growing exurban counties ought to be his mission. He would stand a better chance with that strategy than his current, fruitless crusade.

Ethics: Lax Standards in Annapolis

December 7, 1997

Every few years, the name Joseph J. Staszak reappears in print. It's always for the same reason, too, that the immortal words of the late East Baltimore ward heeler and state senator are given renewed prominence.

Thanks to Larry Young, it's resurrection time once again.

What Staszak said in the early 1970s, while standing on the floor of the Maryland Senate after a morning meeting of that legislative body, concerned a bill he was pushing that would directly increase his tavern's business. He was asked by a reporter if he considered that a conflict of interest.

"Conflict of interest?" he replied quizzically. "How does this conflict with *my* interest?"

Indeed.

Staszak saw nothing wrong in using his legislative position to help put money in his company's bank account. Similarly, state Senator Larry Young of West Baltimore sees nothing wrong in "leveraging" (as he put it himself) his post in Annapolis to benefit companies he has started.

His lapses in ethics are blatant. Blaming it on *Sun* reporters, who wrote the investigative story last week, or on racism won't work. He has put himself and his legislative colleagues in an embarrassing position.

Indeed, Mr. Young's predicament could extend far beyond embarrassment. The state prosecutor is rightly examining evidence to determine if laws were broken. Even if he gets a clean bill of health, Mr. Young still could be stripped of the legislative posts that have provided him with his "leverage."

That is, if legislative leaders recognize the seriousness of Mr. Young's ethical lapses. That could be a problem, since members of the General Assembly's joint ethics committee have rarely come down harshly on their colleagues.

Mr. Young traded on his legislative position to gain fees for his companies

from health-care corporations that do millions in business with the state. He pressed businesses to contribute to his various causes. And he worked out a deal with Coppin State College to serve as a consultant — essentially a lobbyist for Coppin's requests that go before the legislature and the administration.

None of this is new. Senate President Thomas V. Mike Miller has had talks with Mr. Young before about his questionable activities. When he was in the House, Mr. Young was cautioned by House speakers, too. Over the years, Mr. Young has not been shy about pressing lobbyists. And he put his position as chairman of the Executive Nominations Committee to good use as well.

But rarely has any of this received a public airing. Now that it has, Mr. Miller might not be able to let Mr. Young off with a tap on the wrist.

For one thing, exonerating Mr. Young would be tantamount to Mr. Miller saying "everybody does it." Well, "everybody" doesn't do it. But in the public's eyes, failure to discipline a wayward legislator makes all legislators look sleazy.

For another, Mr. Miller cannot let Larry Young become a poster child for Republican Ellen Sauerbrey's crusade to "change the culture in Annapolis."

The longer Mr. Young remains in leadership posts, the more frequently Ms. Sauerbrey will use him to excoriate Democrats.

That could pose a dual danger for Mr. Miller. First, his new-found devotion to Governor Parris N. Glendening might be for naught, since Mr. Glendening is the most likely person to be tied to Mr. Young by the Republicans. Second, if Ms. Sauerbrey successfully uses Mr. Young as Exhibit A in her argument for making a clean sweep of Democrats in Annapolis, she might generate enough voter momentum to endanger Mr. Miller's control of the Senate.

In a large sense, the discomfiture of legislative leaders is deserved. Over the years, lawmakers have failed to set tough standards of conduct for themselves. And they have been even more remiss in failing to set tough enforcement mechanisms. Indeed, lawmakers have consistently denied to the state prosecutor the money and the enforcement statutes he needs to do his job properly.

The notion that a weak, internal legislative ethics committee — which meets in private and never reveals details — can keep legislators on the straight and narrow is a myth propagated by lawmakers themselves.

The Young case could be a turning point for state legislators. Either they get serious about enforcing high ethical standards or they risk infuriating voters as this becomes a prime campaign issue.

Defending the Indefensible

January 25, 1998

Defending the indefensible puts you in an untenable position. That's what Larry Young's supporters may eventually discover. And it is what Maryland farmers may discover in trying to stop the state from mandating how much fertilizer and chicken manure can be applied to their fields.

Look first at Mr. Young's predicament.

He has been expelled from the state Senate for flagrantly using his public office for private gain. The evidence was overwhelming.

He claimed ignorance — after 24 years in the legislature — and portrayed himself as a martyred black politician being crucified by the white power structure in Annapolis. His supporters, many from his own church, say "everybody does it" in the State House, so why pick on a black politician? They also claim he did nothing wrong.

That's a hard sell. He did do something wrong. It was blatant.

He took $34,000 from Coppin State College for doing little more than what he should have been doing as an elected official.

He billed health-care companies for services rendered at exorbitant rates — all the while presiding over health-care bills in the legislature that affect these companies.

All of his Senate colleagues — black as well as white — thought he had engaged in grievous misconduct. They only disagreed over the degree of punishment.

The 46 votes for censure were telling. My Webster's defines "censure" as "condemning as wrong; strong disapproval." Not one senator defended Mr. Young's actions as proper.

That puts clergy in Mr. Young's community on a slippery moral slope in defending the former senator. It should give all his defenders pause.

What he did may or may not be criminal: That is up to the state prosecu-

tor and the U.S. attorney to decide. But the Senate and a joint House-Senate committee unanimously found his actions to be highly unethical. From a moral standpoint, Mr. Young's actions are not something you'd want to hold up as an example of proper behavior. There is a clear difference between right and wrong. Mr. Young boldly crossed the line. It's not even a close call. Even worse, he's been around long enough to know better.

While supporting Mr. Young vociferously may be good for Radio One Inc. owner Cathy Hughes and the profitability of her radio stations, and it may be good for Delegate Clarence M. Mitchell IV, who craves Mr. Young's Senate seat, it does irreparable harm to race relations in the Baltimore region.

Decent, honorable leaders in the black community, like Mayor Kurt L. Schmoke and NAACP president Kweisi Mfume, wind up trying to defend a sleazy, dishonorable character like Mr. Young. They end up defending the indefensible — and demeaning themselves in the process.

Similarly, farmers find themselves defending agricultural practices that honestly cannot be defended.

Nutrient runoffs from farmland, especially phosphorus runoffs, have been scientifically linked to a troubling environmental problem in the Chesapeake Bay — the toxic Pfiesteria scare last summer that almost surely will return this year. Overuse of chicken manure as fertilizer on Eastern Shore farms has contributed mightily to this serious health problem.

How can the farming community rail against efforts in Annapolis to address what is a distressing public-health and environmental problem?

Indeed, it is hard for nonfarmers to understand why all the commotion over a proposal to require nutrient-management plans on all farms. It is shocking that all farmers don't employ such a strategy already. But many do not. A voluntary program won't work.

If the farmers had a viable alternative approach to stemming the phosphorus runoffs and the overuse of chicken manure as fertilizer on the Eastern Shore, they would be on solid ground. The governor's Pfiesteria-prevention program is ripe for revision. But they don't have a plan — other than a return to the status quo.

That's tantamount to opposing efforts to clean up the Chesapeake Bay, or opposing steps to ward off threats to public health. It's the equivalent of opposing motherhood and apple pie. And, like the case of Larry Young's supporters, it's an indefensible position.

His Legacy: the Gold(stein) Standard

July 8, 1998

They buried Louie Goldstein yesterday, and with him ended an era. He was the last state officeholder who served both before and after World War II. But then he also spanned the conflicts in Korea and Vietnam. He was always part of the Annapolis scene.

Louis L. Goldstein dedicated himself to public service. It was his life, and his love. No one had more affection for Maryland. Never did anyone express his devotion so often in so many parts of the state.

Forty years as state comptroller. Sixty years in public service. It was an incredible record that led folks to believe Louie Goldstein would be around forever. But the unthinkable has happened. An institution has vanished from the scene.

You'd have to be eligible for full Social Security benefits to remember a time when you went into the voting booth and did not see Louis Goldstein's name on the ballot for Maryland comptroller.

If you live in Calvert County, you'd have to be 85 to have voted in a state election when Mr. Goldstein's name wasn't on your ballot (except for the four years he was in the Marines).

He was part of our lives. His presence assured us everything was right with the world, that our tax dollars were in good hands, that we could trust our elected leaders.

He served as an anchor for Democrats running for state office. Governor Parris N. Glendening counted on the Goldstein name this year to help his own chances of winning. Even at the age of 85, Mr. Goldstein was deemed so unbeatable that, before his death, no Democrat had filed against him.

Now a mad scramble is on to succeed him. It may have appeared unseemly for candidates to file even as the comptroller's casket lay in the State House. The timing of his death, though, made such a jarring juxtaposition

inevitable. Louis would have understood, and chuckled.

He was, after all, the consummate campaigner, an exemplar of the politics of optimism. He was every bit as much the "Happy Warrior" as another irrepressible Democrat, Hubert Humphrey.

Other politicians came away amazed by his inexhaustible enthusiasm — in private as well as in public. Always upbeat. Delivering hilarious lectures about raising tomatoes or the necessity of changing shoes and socks to keep refreshed.

As a political realist, he would relish the race to succeed him. Even in death, he casts a huge shadow. Everything his successor does will be judged against the Gold(stein) Standard.

Depending on the results in November, Mr. Goldstein's passing may also signal the end of another era — Democratic control of state government.

Without him on the Democratic ticket, the party may lose the governorship, letting a Republican draw new districts for the state legislature and Congress. That could prove the turning point for Maryland's outnumbered GOP.

There were two sides to Mr. Goldstein. Outside his office, he was a smiling and happy celebrity, whose joy never waned while mingling with citizens.

Bureaucrats and elected leaders saw the other side: a hard-nosed conservative who acted as fiscal watchdog on the powerful Board of Public Works.

Mr. Goldstein was never a rubber stamp. He often opposed governors on proposals he felt frivolous or ill-conceived.

He terrorized bureaucrats at board meetings. It helped that he practically memorized voluminous back-up material and visited project sites. You couldn't buffalo Mr. Goldstein.

He had the good sense to promote capable professionals in the comptroller's office and let them run the show. Yet he was a stickler for modernizing tax collections.

It's astonishing that no one ever blamed Louie Goldstein for the taxes he or she owed. His popularity soared even as he cheerfully asked folks to send in their tax dollars early ("Don't delay, file today") so they could get quick refunds.

It was a superb gimmick. People felt better about their government after hearing a Goldstein pep talk or funny story.

They adored his fast-talking spiel, with that thick Southern Maryland accent. They trusted him with their money. And they loved him for his stability.

Marylanders knew that as long as Louie Goldstein was around, everything would work out all right in Annapolis.

That certainty has now been removed. With 19 candidates filing for comptroller, the post-Goldstein era begins with state politics in flux.

Life without Louie won't be easy.

Chapter 9

Electing
a New
Governor

Speak Only Ill of a Fellow Republican

December 8, 1996

Those wacky Republicans are at it again. There's never a dull moment inside the Maryland GOP, also known as the gang that can't shoot straight. A deep divide separates factions within the party. And because their differences are so basic, don't look for a truce.

On the one side sit the True Believers. They are fundamental conservatives, both in theory and in practice — purists who brook no deviations and abhor compromise. Their devotion to the cause at times borders on fanaticism.

Blended into this group are die-hard fiscal conservatives as well as Christian Right social conservatives. To them, keeping faith with their beliefs is more important than passing legislation or even winning elections.

On the other side reside the Pragmatists. Many are conservative, but they're not zealots. They follow Ronald Reagan's "big tent" approach — be flexible and tolerant enough to accommodate a vast array of political viewpoints.

This side believes that a democracy can work well only if there is a willingness to seek consensus among the clamor of voices. Moderation is no vice, they maintain, in crafting legislation or executive policy.

True Believers adamantly disagree. Moderation is a vice. Only by preaching and practicing a purist form of conservatism can the country be saved.

At the moment, Maryland's True Believers have elevated their standard bearer, Ellen R. Sauerbrey, to near-sainthood. Anyone who disagrees or opposes her is castigated as "liberal" and accused of treason.

In recent weeks, though, Howard County Executive Charles I. Ecker and former Anne Arundel County Executive Robert R. Neall — staunch fiscal conservatives — emerged as Pragmatists who might challenge Ms. Sauerbrey for dominance of the state GOP. True Believers went into a frenzy.

Mr. Neall was accused of being "liberal" and a tool of Democrats. Mr. Ecker was called a pseudo-conservative and a "get along, go along" politician. Even the late state Senator John A. Cade was pilloried as an impure conservative who dared work with Democrats.

And now True Believers have turned on Anne Arundel County Executive John G. Gary. His sin? Daring to express the well-known fact that when he and Ms. Sauerbrey served in the General Assembly, her views were often out of sync with lawmakers, including some within her own party.

That kind of talk isn't acceptable. So Mr. Gary was taken to the woodshed by Ms. Sauerbrey and one of her chief supporters, businessman Richard E. Hug. They don't want GOP dissension.

Not everyone in the state party, though, is willing to cede control to the True Believers.

Pragmatists maintain that Ms. Sauerbrey could lead the party to disaster. Yes, she came within an eyelash of winning the governorship in 1994, but that was due to the weakness of the Democratic nominee, not the public's embrace of her conservatism.

In a rerun, these Republicans feel a golden opportunity could be lost. Ms. Sauerbrey remains too hard-edged to defeat even an unpopular Governor Parris N. Glendening. These Republicans want a centrist candidate, such as Mr. Ecker, who could draw disenchanted Democratic voters.

True Believers hold the opposite view. Marylanders want a choice, not an echo, they argue. Only a pure conservative like Ms. Sauerbrey fits the bill. She cannot lose against a weakened Mr. Glendening in 1998.

This struggle within the Maryland Republican Party is not new. It is a continuation of the decades-old tug of war between the left and right wings.

At the moment, the right wing has the upper hand. Ms. Sauerbrey soundly defeated the moderates' choice, Helen D. Bentley, in the 1994 primary, and almost won the general election.

But coming close only wins at horseshoes. History shows that centrist Republicans are far more likely to be victorious than right-wingers in Maryland.

Since World War II, voters have repeatedly rejected hardened conservatives in statewide races — the main exception being John Marshall Butler, who won by using "Red scare" smear tactics against a four-term conservative Democratic U.S. Senator, Millard Tydings.

Which side will gain control of the party? It may take a showdown in the 1998 GOP primary to decide. Even then, failure to win the governorship could re-ignite the controversy as Maryland Republicans continue to search for their true identity.

John Gary made peace with Ellen Sauerbrey and served as co-chairman of her 1998 gubernatorial campaign.

It Was a Risk – So Cardin Declined

September 7, 1997

In the end, it came down to a matter of desire. As Walter Mondale might have put it, Ben Cardin lacked the "fire in the belly" to run for governor. So Mr. Cardin, who loomed large over the gubernatorial race, will remain in Congress while others try to dislodge Governor Parris Glendening.

The Baltimore-area congressman acted according to form. A decade ago, he tried running for governor and withdrew after he realized it might be an "iffy" proposition. Ben Cardin is someone who doesn't like to take chances. Never having faced a tough campaign in 30 years, Mr. Cardin was not about to start. Governor Glendening understood that perhaps better than anyone: He applied enough pressure to make the congressman nervous.

Mr. Cardin's history is instructive. He was appointed to the House of Delegates in 1967, while still in law school, to replace his uncle, who had been named a judge. It was a political deal worked out in advance.

He quietly rose in prominence, thanks to his brilliance, his mastery of the legislative process and his city and family ties. He was always in the right place: heir-apparent to the Ways and Means Committee chairmanship when Delegate John Hanson Briscoe moved up to the speakership, heir-apparent to the speakership when Mr. Briscoe was named a judge; heir-apparent to a congressional seat when Barbara Mikulski moved to the U.S. Senate from the House of Representatives in 1986.

He maneuvered behind the scenes to make it happen without a public fight. That's what he tried this time, but it didn't work. As he conceded afterward, it was "not my kind of race."

Ben Cardin is the consummate back-room, consensus politician. He likes to flesh everything out beforehand. No public controversies or cliff-hanger votes. In eight years as House speaker in Annapolis, he never lost a vote — and rarely had a close call.

He's never been in a hotly contested campaign, either, and never has Mr. Cardin taken on a task as daunting as challenging an incumbent governor of his own party. "I don't like to be out of control," he remarked.

Yet in a governor's race, it is nearly impossible to control events, especially when running against an incumbent. It takes an adept, flexible and fearless politician to make such a race.

Mr. Cardin mapped out a strategy and he refused to deviate from it: Spend a summer canvassing leading Democrats and making fund-raising plans; then declare his candidacy in the fall with the early backing of the state's top four local officials, thus gaining instant credibility.

That plan, Mr. Cardin now admits, was "naive," because it depended on early endorsements from Baltimore Mayor Kurt L. Schmoke and county executives Dutch Ruppersberger (Baltimore County), Douglas Duncan (Montgomery County) and Wayne Curry (Prince George's County). It proved a stunning miscalculation.

Messrs. Schmoke, Ruppersberger, Curry and Duncan cannot afford to alienate the governor at this stage. They still have to deal with him throughout next January's General Assembly session. Openly supporting an opponent now would have been suicidal.

When Mr. Cardin broached the notion of a unified, four-pronged endorsement at the Maryland Association of Counties meeting last month, these officials were aghast. They told him it couldn't — and wouldn't — happen.

From that point on, Mr. Cardin's ardor waned.

The governor's efforts also played a role. The congressman wondered if the early endorsements of Mr. Glendening by black city and P.G. lawmakers would damage his vote strength in these communities. And he worried that the governor could dilute Cardin support in Montgomery County by portraying the congressman as a tax-raising Baltimore pol.

Things were spinning out of his control. But rather than change his strategy to accommodate the wishes of the four local officials (they would have endorsed him in the spring had Mr. Cardin launched his campaign then), the congressman took the easy route out of the race.

This might end his hopes for higher elective office. A horde of Democrats will be running for governor in 2002 — including Mr. Duncan and Mr. Ruppersberger. Democratic Senator Paul Sarbanes shows no sign of retiring in 2000, either.

An old lottery slogan proclaimed, "You've gotta play to win." The same holds true for high elective office: You've got to get in the race, and stay there, if you want a chance to win.

Spiro Agnew did it in 1966 as a decided underdog, and won. Harry Hughes did it against all odds in 1978, and won. William Donald Schaefer did it in 1986, and won. Parris Glendening bucked prevailing sentiment in 1994, and won.

None of them faced an easy race or a sure thing. All of them took a huge risk — the sort of risk Mr. Cardin was unwilling to take.

Will Voters Look For Fresh Horses?

November 2, 1997

If Chuck Ecker and Eileen Rehrmann were running for re-election as county executive in Howard and Harford counties, respectively, they would be considered prohibitive favorites.

But they are limited by law to two terms. So these two successful politicians instead are running for governor — not as favorites but decided underdogs.

Republican Ecker officially plunged into the GOP race this past week; Democrat Rehrmann did so the week before. He has by far the more difficult challenge.

For state Republicans — wandering in the gubernatorial wilderness for 30 years — 1998 looks like a breakthrough. But not for Charles I. Ecker. GOP leaders are rallying around Ellen R. Sauerbrey, who came within 6,000 votes of becoming governor in 1994.

Ms. Sauerbrey has never stopped running. She is lionized by party conservatives who swear she was robbed through ballot-box chicanery. Other Republicans feel she deserves a second shot.

Polls show her far ahead of Mr. Ecker. He has his work cut out.

It is not impossible. Mr. Ecker pulled off a shocker to become Howard County's first elected Republican executive in 1990. Ms. Sauerbrey won the 1994 GOP nomination in a huge upset. Both Harry R. Hughes (Democratic primary, 1978) and socialite Louise Gore (Republican primary, 1974) stunned heavy favorites.

Mr. Ecker tried last week to draw distinctions between himself and Ms. Sauerbrey: She lacks compassion, she's trying to win with the same tired themes, she has no management experience, she can't work with Democrats.

He must find issues where differences are compelling. Perhaps education, where Mr. Ecker will propose a new funding formula for $2 billion in state aid. Ms. Sauerbrey is a fan of reducing future state spending, not increasing it.

They differ on job development, too. Ms. Sauerbrey believes you attract businesses by sharply lowering the state income tax. Republican Governor Christine Whitman has tried that in New Jersey; now she is fighting for survival in Tuesday's election. By contrast, Mr. Ecker has attracted businesses to Howard through traditional means.

His biggest advantage, though, could be Ms. Sauerbrey's low popularity ratings among registered Democrats. Mr. Ecker must persuade Republicans that Ms. Sauerbrey will take the party down the road to defeat, continuing the Democrats' hegemony.

He contends that in a general election, where Republicans are outnumbered 2-1, you cannot win with a staunch conservative.

Yet he starts his campaign far behind, with little organization or cash. But money may not be a decisive factor. With all the campaign financing abuses being aired in Washington, any candidate who raises huge sums may be suspect.

That could help Eileen Rehrmann, thanks to Governor Parris N. Glendening's habit of squeezing special-interest groups for donations. Voters might view this as trying to buy the election.

Her early literature takes subtle digs at the governor. She reminds voters she served as a state legislator; many of the governor's problems stem from his lack of General Assembly experience.

She touts her "sound financial management," alluding to the $100 million debt Mr. Glendening left behind in Prince George's County. She trumpets national recognition for Harford's economic development efforts.

But where is the cutting-edge issue? She is hoping that by the end of the General Assembly session in mid-April, a few hot-button controversies will emerge.

Ms. Rehrmann is raising a surprisingly large amount of money for a long shot. She pulled off a big coup in winning the active backing of Larry S. Gibson, one of the state's top political strategists and campaign organizers.

But her biggest edge could be the mirror image of what Mr. Ecker is counting on: a growing sense of disaster among Democratic politicians of a Glendening-Sauerbrey match-up. Mr. Glendening just isn't wildly popular.

Senate President Mike Miller is running scared, alarmed that a Sauerbrey triumph in many suburbs could cost Democrats control of the Senate. Some leading Democrats share Mr. Miller's concern, and blame Mr. Glendening.

But only one of the two scenarios — Mr. Ecker's vision of Republicans flocking to him in fear of the GOP getting clobbered with Ms. Sauerbrey as the nominee or Ms. Rehrmann's picture of a Democratic debacle under Mr. Glendening — can come true.

If either of these long-shot contenders can make a persuasive case for their doom-and-gloom scenario, we could have a major surprise next September 15. But it would take a tremendous amount of hard work — and considerable good fortune — for that to happen.

Rehrmann's Tax-cut Idea

November 23, 1997

Chalk one up for Eileen Rehrmann. The two-term Harford county executive jump-started her 1998 campaign for governor this past week and in the process sent a resounding message to Governor Parris N. Glendening that he faces an aggressive, creative opponent in the Democratic primary.

Her call for eliminating the state property tax suddenly puts this heretofore unnoticed issue on the legislature's agenda. It is a new twist on the 1994 tax-cut proposal of Republican candidate Ellen Sauerbrey that almost got her elected.

But there are sharp differences. Ms. Sauerbrey's proposal for a 24-percent income-tax reduction would have required sweeping budget cuts and would have left the state in a deep deficit crater as soon as the good economic times turn to recession. Her Republican plan also could not be accomplished without the Democratic legislature altering the income-tax law — an unlikely prospect.

In contrast, Ms. Rehrmann's property-tax rollback would cost only a fraction of the Sauerbrey plan. The governor can do it without General Assembly approval. And it contains an important safety net for the state: Any future governor, at his or her discretion, could opt to reinstate the Maryland property tax levy to help balance a future budget.

While the Rehrmann camp would love this issue to propel their candidate directly into the governor's mansion, it won't happen that way.

Maryland is different from Virginia, where Republican James Gilmore's call to end the hated personal property tax on cars made the difference in that state's recent election for governor.

What Ms. Rehrmann gains from her tax plan is vastly increased visibility and prestige. She, not the governor, has now set the agenda. Indeed, Mr. Glendening finds himself — for the moment — on the defensive.

Does he ignore the Rehrmann proposal in his budget and hand her a tailor-made campaign issue next summer?

Or does he defuse this issue by embracing a portion of her tax-rollback plan, though this could validate Ms. Rehrmann's fiscal expertise for voters? Either way, the governor winds up helping his Democratic primary opponent. He's been outmaneuvered.

Taxes will play some role in the campaign. Latest estimates indicate a state surplus of at least $311 million this fiscal year. Spending that money — for school construction or health programs or tax rebates — will be much discussed during the General Assembly session that starts in January.

Ms. Sauerbrey still is pushing her 1994 program. She urges the governor to accelerate his 2-percent-a-year income-tax reduction with much of that surplus cash. A high income-tax rate remains "one of the biggest drags on business development," she said last week.

To date, Mr. Glendening has taken a prudent course on taxes and on spending. But with such a huge surplus on hand, he may have to come up with another tax-reduction plan in early 1998 to mute the Rehrmann and Sauerbrey challenges.

At a breakfast meeting with business leaders last week in Baltimore, the two candidates for governor demonstrated beyond question that Mr. Glendening faces two tough, tenacious foes.

Ms. Rehrmann's tax-cut surprise may be the start of a primary campaign filled with surprises designed to keep Mr. Glendening off-guard and to raise public acceptance of the Harford county executive.

Republicans, meanwhile, have reason to cheer Ms. Sauerbrey's polished performances before business and community groups. She comes off sounding gubernatorial in outlining a sweeping array of changes she would make in Annapolis.

Voters may yet decide to keep the governor they already know rather than the candidate they don't fully trust.

Good economic times may do the trick for Mr. Glendening. Historically, this is a state of "middle temperament," whose citizens seem to like prudent moderates with a mildly progressive streak.

But Governor Glendening won't have an easy time in 1998. Eileen Rehrmann's property-tax broadside last week and Ellen Sauerbrey's ongoing conservative crusade to "change the long-standing culture in Annapolis" could haunt him all year.

Eilenn Rehrmann's property tax proposal never gained support in the General Assembly. The state's rejuvenated economy, though, led to an acceleration of the governor's income-tax cut, just as Ellen Sauerbrey had suggested.

Glendening Fails to Capture Spotlight

February 1, 1998

It wasn't supposed to work like this. By now, Governor Parris N. Glendening should be riding high in the polls, after a carefully orchestrated effort to raise his visibility and his popularity.

This is, after all, the time of year when any Maryland governor should sparkle. The State of the State address, the high point of the governor's policy pronouncements, is the only time a governor gets to address Marylanders in a full-fledged, televised speech lasting close to an hour.

Mr. Glendening had carefully dribbled out tasty morsels of his election-year program in recent months. With his January 22 speech, he was the center of attention, a political hero doling out millions for social programs that people care about.

But then came scandals revolving around state Senator Larry Young and Bill Clinton. Mr. Glendening, instead of being in the spotlight, was shoved into the background.

In most years, he'd dominate the front page with his big speech; this year, Mr. Glendening was shoved off the page entirely.

He didn't even get the lead in *The Sun's* Metro section; the article on his speech ran beneath the fold. He lost out to such stories as "Clinton goes on air, denies new charges," "Castro, Cubans warmly welcome 'pilgrim of hope,' " "Planners to vote on Angelos' hotel," even "Kelley is catching some criticism for her lone abstention on Young."

"We can't catch a break," moaned an aide to Mr. Glendening.

The governor's bad luck was magnified by the release of a Mason-Dixon Maryland poll showing Mr. Glendening in a virtual dead heat with Republican Ellen R. Sauerbrey. He remains one of the nation's most vulnerable governors, with high negatives.

As Mason-Dixon President Brad Coker put it, "It would seem that

Glendening has tried every political move to restore his popularity, but it just doesn't seem to happen." Whatever he does, "he appears to get no credit." The problem, Mr. Coker concludes, is "the issue of trust. Voters perceived his motives as purely political — taken only as a matter of convenience to win re-election."

That public unease toward Mr. Glendening has only been magnified by the Young scandal and the brewing Clinton sex expose. The Young affair has the most direct impact on him. The governor, after all, had allied himself closely with Mr. Young to generate a big vote in Baltimore. And Mr. Young apparently was one of the key players in a major fund-raiser for the governor in New York at the home of a health-care executive bidding for a giant state contract at the time.

Even worse for the governor, he seems caught in a dilemma: He wants to remain on Mr. Young's good side, in order to retain his standing in Baltimore's black communities. So he has evaded any denunciation of the deplorable, unethical behavior that led to Mr. Young's expulsion from the state Senate.

But that just makes Mr. Glendening look like a craven politician to most of middle Maryland, where Mr. Young is viewed as a prime example of political sleaze. If the governor won't denounce such behavior, *ipso facto*, he must condone some or all of what Mr. Young has done.

That just plays into Ms. Sauerbrey's hands. Count on her campaign to tie the governor to Mr. Young this summer and fall, especially if Mr. Young runs for his former Senate seat. What happens if Mr. Young wins the Democratic primary, which seems highly likely? Mr. Glendening will have to support the Democratic nominee, or risk severe damage to his vote total in a key constituency — black voters in Baltimore. That makes it all the easier for Ms. Sauerbrey to lump Glendening-Young as "birds of a feather" all stuck together.

Already, Ms. Sauerbrey is harping on the need for "a culture change" in Annapolis. She will continue to sound the theme that the Democrats' stranglehold in the state capital has led to a decline in ethical standards.

Feeding into that rhetoric is the decline of moral standards in the White House. How convenient for Republican Sauerbrey that Mr. Young and Mr. Clinton, both Democrats, happened onto the scene. She can seize the moral and ethical high ground and demonstrate the need for a clean sweep in Annapolis, starting with the Democratic governor.

Neither the Young saga nor the Clinton saga will disappear soon. That is bad news for Mr. Glendening: Getting the Maryland voting public to focus on substantive government achievements — his top political goal — could turn into a Herculean undertaking.

Larry Young decided not to file for reelection to the state Senate.

With Schaefer Bid, All Bets Are Off

July 10, 1998

Cast Robert Redford in a movie and you have box-office success. Cast Liza Minnelli in a Broadway musical and every performance is standing-room only.

Bring back William Donald Schaefer for a starring role in a statewide election and public attention is riveted on him.

No one else in Maryland has the charisma and showmanship of the ex-governor, ex-mayor and ex-retiree. What had all the appearances of a drab election campaign now crackles with excitement.

That's a relief after the deadly serious — and oh so bland — patter from Governor Parris N. Glendening, his chief GOP rival Ellen R. Sauerbrey and his chief Democratic tormentor, Eileen M. Rehrmann.

In just four days, Mr. Schaefer eclipsed them all by filing for a lesser statewide office — state comptroller — a move that precipitated the resignation yesterday of the interim comptroller hand-picked by the governor on Monday.

Democratic candidates for governor are now jumping through hoops to ingratiate themselves with Mr. Schaefer. He has become the kingpin and they know it.

What Mr. Schaefer seeks to do — escape from a retirement he dislikes intensely to start a second state career — has only one near-parallel in Maryland annals.

J. Millard Tawes, after two terms as governor (and 17 years previously as comptroller) thought he had finished his public service in 1966.

But three years later, Governor Marvin Mandel asked Tawes to return to play peacemaker as secretary of the newly consolidated Department of Natural Resources.

In 1971, Tawes retired again — until a scandal forced the state treasurer to resign. When the governor and legislators asked him in 1973 to shape up that office, the 79-year-old Tawes obliged.

He left for good in 1975 as he neared his 81st birthday.

By those standards, the 76-year-old Donald Schaefer is still in the prime of political life. He's three years younger than was Tawes when he was brought back as state treasurer and nine years younger than was Mr. Goldstein in what turned out to be his final year as comptroller.

To the public, the Schaefer name is magic.

Those who were angry at him during his tenure as governor have forgotten the Schaefer tantrums and rages. Instead, they recall the colorful zaniness of a guy who reminds them of the late Louie Goldstein, Maryland's beloved comptroller for the past 40 years.

They recall other similarities, too: an unflinching devotion to government service, a true love affair with Maryland citizens, a streak of stubborn independence, rock-solid integrity, and a commitment to do right by voters.

Mr. Schaefer's determination to stay in the race created a nightmare for Michael D. Barnes, the star-crossed ex-congressman picked by Mr. Glendening to fill out Mr. Goldstein's term and run on the Glendening ticket.

What looked like an easy romp for Mr. Barnes on Monday afternoon turned into a terrifying, uphill trek when Mr. Schaefer signed his filing papers that evening.

No wonder Mr. Barnes beat a hasty — and embarrassing — retreat. He would have been routed in a campaign against an ex-governor who has a deep reservoir of good will and renown in every corner of this state.

Thus, Mr. Barnes resigned the post he had just assumed, setting a record for the shortest tenure by a Maryland comptroller in the 146-year history of that office.

What a stunning and totally unexpected comeback by William Donald Schaefer. Those who opt to remain in the comptroller's race face a humiliating defeat in September and then in November against such a formidable candidate. Celebrity politicians hold enormous appeal with voters.

Mr. Schaefer's re-emergence on the political stage, after a four-year absence, alters the dynamics of gubernatorial politics this year. Here is what could well happen:

Mr. Schaefer could provide coattail power from below for the Democratic nominee for governor in November, dooming Ms. Sauerbrey's chances.

With Louie Goldstein's death, Maryland voters will be looking for stability in state government. William Donald Schaefer appeals to many citizens for that reason.

He is the elder statesman, after all, with a larger-than-life reputation for rejuvenating Baltimore and then governing Maryland with exuberance for two terms.

The present governor needs Mr. Schaefer's help. His misguided dalliance with Mr. Barnes — and his initial refusal to consider Mr. Schaefer for the

interim comptroller's job — leaves him with egg on his face. It was a dreadful political miscalculation. Even worse, Mr. Glendening is wide open to charges of politicizing the comptroller's office by naming his campaign chairman to the post. And by pushing Mr. Barnes out the door just after he arrived, Mr. Glendening once again looks like a crass opportunist, a supreme flip-flopper — the ultimate survivalist.

How badly Mr. Glendening is hurt by this comedy of errors depends on his opponents' abilities to capitalize on his misfortunes. Both Ms. Rehrmann and Ms. Sauerbrey will use the Barnes fiasco against him. But it is Mr. Schaefer who can make or break Mr. Glendening. The governor must stay on his good side or risk more trouble.

With his immense public appeal and celebrity status, William Donald Schaefer is once again the center of attention, the centerfold of the 1998 political season. It is a phenomenon without precedent in this state's long history.

Pragmatic Sauerbrey Steers to Center

July 26, 1998

Introducing the "new" Ellen Sauerbrey. Not the tough, doctrinaire conservative who barely missed becoming governor in 1994 (and then loudly complained she had been robbed), but the soft, pragmatic Republican running for vindication this year.

Yes, it's a kinder, gentler Ellen Sauerbrey. She's better financed and more sophisticated. She wants voters to know she has matured, thought about what it would mean to be governor and has moderated her stands accordingly.

Yet underneath this gloss, her bedrock principles remain firm, attached like concrete to a conservative philosophy. The "new" Ms. Sauerbrey offers voters a more vibrant package, but basically the same ingredients.

Her strength is also her greatest weakness. Recent polls show that roughly one-third of voters look upon her favorably, but another third have an unfavorable view. The rest are undecided. She stirs passions.

The most recent polls indicate another exceedingly close race, with Governor Parris N. Glendening just 7 points ahead in the Mason-Dixon poll and 6 points ahead in the Potomac Survey Research poll. To close that gap, Ms. Sauerbrey needs to broaden her support beyond registered Republicans and conservative independents.

That helps explain the new Sauerbrey appeal to centrists. Why else would she choose moderate Richard D. Bennett as her running mate over Paul H. Rappaport, the darling of conservatives?

Why else would she endorse for comptroller Michael Steele, a little-known African American from Prince George's County, infuriating her right-wing backers?

Why is she making well-publicized forays into black communities in Baltimore? She seeks to chip away at Mr. Glendening's base. That also

explains why she is focusing on populous Montgomery County, another Glendening stronghold.

The trick is to make Ms. Sauerbrey sound gubernatorial, without the hard edges of 1994.

Tax cut? Yes, she stands by her proposed 24 percent reduction from last time, but now wants this achieved over four years — not in one massive billion-dollar swipe.

Incentives to attract jobs? Cut red tape first. As for big state grants to firms, she would restrict them to out-of-state companies and smaller businesses. No corporate welfare for big companies.

Aid for Baltimore? To prove she's not hostile, she is stressing her city roots. But she isn't an urban big-spender. Her stress is on revitalizing the city's "merchant class" (small businesses), hardly a large-ticket item.

Crime? She's a hard-liner who talks of stemming drug use, educating kids to the dangers, finding out which treatment programs are effective and getting urban churches more involved.

Education? She doesn't mention large aid increases to underperforming schools. Instead, she talks of "putting resources in the classroom," i.e., making school management lean. She talks of better testing to identify young kids with learning problems and giving local elected officials audit powers over school spending.

The Sauerbrey approach calls for smaller government that demands greater accountability, slimmed down management and narrowly targeted objectives. It requires fewer taxes and less government regulation.

Less doctrinaire this time. Take school vouchers. She says she has changed her approach, recognizing the reality that the governor's primary role is to strengthen public education, not promote private schools. Instead, she favors tax credits to give parents a choice. A different slant, but the outcome may be the same.

She is trying to look pragmatic. For instance, she flatly opposes casinos, but might approve some slot-machines at race tracks, directing revenues to save the thoroughbred industry. First, though, she says the state should try other options — better marketing, televising major stakes races and a huge Preakness promotion. There would be "no handouts or grants," but possibly long-term, low-interest loans for track renovations.

It is a new Ellen Sauerbrey in many respects. She understands that she must make amends for the whining, "sour grapes" image she created in 1994. She understands she must persuade voters she has matured, that she now understands Governor Sauerbrey would have to be more open-minded, not as dogmatic.

She can win this election. But she must make a convincing case to the bulk of Maryland voters in the political center, the moderates of both parties. Never before has Ms. Sauerbrey zeroed in on them. She has to this time.

Quietly Meeting His Goals

August 2, 1998

They don't love Parris in the springtime; will they love him in the fall?
Probably not. Governor Parris N. Glendening isn't a cuddly politician. He
isn't someone voters swoon over.

But Mr. Glendening is not looking for the electorate's love and adoration,
just its support in his re-election bid. He's running on his impressive record,
not his robotic personality.

To many Marylanders, Parris Nelson Glendening remains a man cloaked in
mystery. They know he's governor, but they don't have a sense of who he is.

He zealously protects his personal life. His childhood in Florida, in
impoverished circumstances, was a tightly guarded secret until recent investigative news articles shed sympathetic light on the subject.

In small groups, he loosens up a bit, even cracks some jokes. Before large
groups, the mechanical man returns — all business, all policy stuff.

He was a dull professor of political science at College Park, students say,
and he's a dull governor. But does that matter?

Mr. Glendening is betting that it doesn't. So far in his career, his calcula-
tion has been proven right. For more than 25 years, he has run and won elections, governed with all the excitement of a soggy bowl of cereal and yet
been re-elected.

His first term as governor is a perfect example of the Glendening
approach. He alienated state legislators on a host of issues by failing to con-
sult frequently with them, by taking most of the credit for legislative work,
by not living up to agreements made in private meetings.

Yet none of this counts in the final analysis. It's all part of the sound and
fury leading to the promulgation of laws and the running of government.

In the end, citizens witnessed a veritable blizzard of progressive legislation and social programs.

Four years ago, he issued a 50-page campaign booklet, "A Vision for Maryland's Future," focusing on "the five E's" — education, law enforcement, the environment, excellence in government and economic development.

He has lived up to or exceeded nearly every one of the pledges on those 50 pages. That's what he will be reminding voters of this fall.

He has been a highly flexible governor. Critics view this as a weakness. They say he has no core beliefs other than furthering his political career. They say every step he takes is carefully calibrated to advance his future.

Yet flexibility is essential in government these days. A rigid, ideological purist in the governor's chair won't get very far with a legislature full of pragmatic pols.

Yes, Mr. Glendening yielded often to legislative demands and accepted sweeping revisions of his bills. But what emerged met the governor's bottom-line objectives.

His task now is to persuade an uninterested and cynical public that the Glendening years have been a time of quiet progress and growing financial stability. He must convince voters that he has been a prudent financial steward but also a governor willing to take courageous stands.

He starts with a handicap.

Voters still remember the dreadful initial months of the Glendening administration — news reports of a looming $100 million deficit he had left behind in Prince George's County; a lucrative pension plan for his aides and himself in Prince George's; cabinet appointments for two of the main architects of that sweetheart pension deal.

It was a bumbling start and, in the eyes of many Marylanders, Mr. Glendening has never recovered.

But this governor is single-minded. He hasn't let those stumbles or other flubs get in his way. He has slowly built an impressive Democratic alliance of elected leaders for the September 15 primary. Harford County Executive Eileen M. Rehrmann, far behind in the polls, may not be able to compete.

If nothing else, Mr. Glendening is a cold-eyed realist. After the primary, he says, Rehrmann defectors will unite behind the Democratic nominee. You don't have to like a candidate to work for his re-election, he says. Given the alternative — a very conservative Republican in Ellen R. Sauerbrey, who has never worked well with Democrats — party leaders will line up rapidly behind him, he predicts.

Then it is a matter of getting out the message that his cumulative record in Annapolis has been an exemplary one, worthy of a second term in office.

Dull is good, he will tell voters, as long as you get positive results.

Eileen Rehrmann disbanded her campaign for governor on August 10, 1998.

Maryland's Ideological Showdown

September 20, 1998

They are bookends on the political spectrum, exemplars of their respective party's ideologies — Parris Glendening on the liberal left, Ellen Sauerbrey on the conservative right.

They clashed four years ago — and finished in nearly a dead heat. It is time for the rematch. Showdown at the OK Corral. Return of the Jedi. Yin versus yang.

They don't have much respect for each other: They are diametric opposites on most everything.

Now that the preliminaries are over — Mr. Glendening won the Democratic primary with 70 percent of the vote, Ms. Sauerbrey gained 81 percent of the Republican primary vote — it could get tense. And nasty.

Which candidate better represents Marylanders' views on key social issues? Which candidate do they trust to run the state?

The two have radically different approaches to government.

A second Glendening term would be an extension of his efforts to extend social programs to the poor and the young. He wants to revive his earlier free-tuition plan for all college-age students and expand free health care to more middle-class families.

Mr. Glendening sees government as a force for good. He is especially committed to improving education. That would include steps to bolster academics at the University of Maryland's flagship College Park campus, where he once taught political science.

It might not be exciting. Incremental progress would remain the Glendening style. But it would be a predictable style.

Not so in a Sauerbrey administration. Her victory would signal the start of a Republican revolution here. For the first time in 32 years, the GOP would control this state's most powerful office.

Conservatives would be named to the judiciary and key regulatory bodies such as the Public Service Commission and the State Board of Education. A conservative Cabinet would run government activities with a business-oriented style. Red tape and regulations would be trimmed to the bone.

First on the Sauerbrey agenda would be tax cuts, supported in the first year by the state's big surplus. She firmly believes this would spur economic growth.

In later years, sharply lower income-tax receipts would require dramatic cuts in state programs. Ms. Sauerbrey has longed for such an opportunity. The Calvert Institute, a thinly veiled arm of the Sauerbrey campaign, has published a 75-page report filled with ways to slash government spending.

There would be wholesale consolidation of departments and agencies. A zero-based budgeting approach would force bureaucrats to justify their existence.

Ms. Sauerbrey — despite her moderating tone of recent months — promises to give Maryland government the most radical transformation in half a century.

Thousands of longtime state managers would depart — replaced by Republicans with determined conservative agendas but little Annapolis experience.

Maryland's constitution grants the governor enormous budgetary powers. Ms. Sauerbrey knows she could cut deeply into existing programs without worrying about General Assembly interference. The legislature can cut, but not increase, a governor's spending program.

Dealing with a heavily Democratic legislature on other matters could be perilous, though. The governor might try to use the bully pulpit to pressure lawmakers to see things her way.

Even a Democratic majority on the three-member Board of Public Works might not pose much of a threat to Ms. Sauerbrey. After all, it's the governor who sets the board's agenda, not the Democratic board members.

Politically, Ms. Sauerbrey intends to accelerate GOP gains in the legislature when she draws new legislative boundaries. Her aim: More districts that favor Republicans. This means far fewer Baltimore senators and delegates.

That is the opposite of what Mr. Glendening would try to achieve: Despite his disputes with Mayor Kurt Schmoke, he would want to retain the city's legislative strength through shared city-county districts.

Rarely have the options been so crystal clear for voters. This election highlights the conflicting emotions found in Maryland's growing suburbs. Residents are torn between their desire for costly government services — good roads, quality education and ample public protection — and their desire to reduce government intrusion in their lives.

Maryland's long tradition of political moderation may be about to change. Or voters may decide to keep the ship of state moving in the same old direction.

The race for governor reflects a national struggle going on in Washington and in other state capitals. But few states offer such a watershed election this year. If there are trends set in 1998, look to them to be set in Maryland.